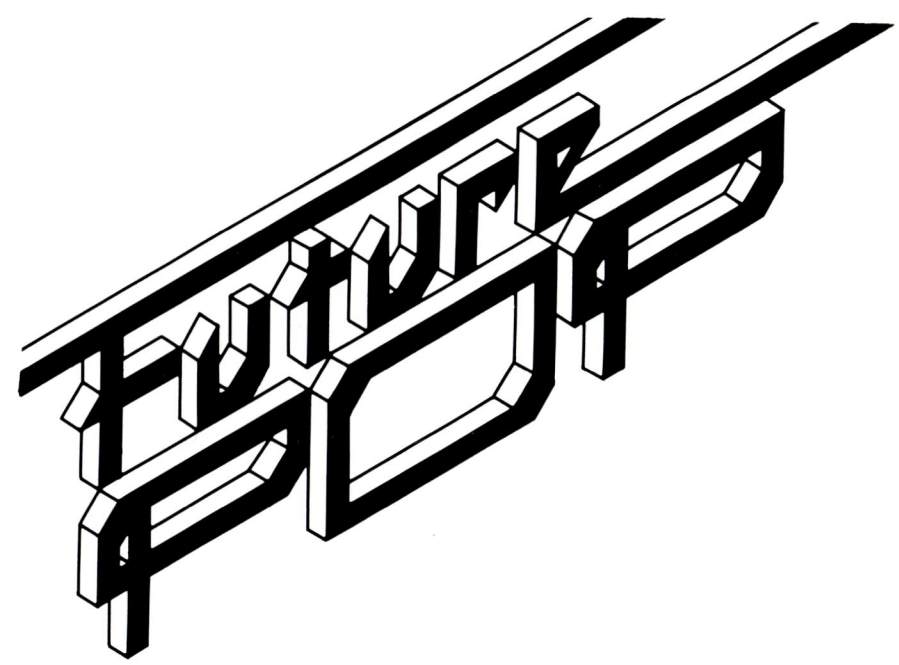

MUSIC FOR THE EIGHTIES
Peter L. Noble

MUSSON/*Toronto*
A member of the General Publishing Group

Design/ Mark Krawczynski

Copyright © 1983 by Peter L. Noble

All rights reserved. No part of this publication may be reproduced or transmitted in any form or by any means, electronic or mechanical, including photocopy, recording, or any information storage or retrieval system now known or to be invented without permission in writing from the publisher, except by a reviewer who wishes to quote brief passages in connection with a review written for inclusion in a magazine, newspaper, or broadcast.

First published in 1983 by
Musson Book Company
A Division of General Publishing Co. Limited
30 Lesmill Road
Toronto, Ontario
M3B 2T6

Canadian Cataloguing in Publication Data
Noble, Peter, 1958-
Future pop: Music for the eighties

ISBN 0-7737-1062-0

1. Rock groups. 2. Rock musicians — Biography.
I. Title

ML3534.N62   784.5'4'00922   C83-094140-1

Printed and bound in Canada

CONTENTS

Acknowledgements 5
Introduction 7

THE ARTISTS

Simple Minds	8	Bow Wow Wow	52
Thompson Twins	10	Gabi Delgado	54
Fad Gadget	12	Psychedelic Furs	55
Bauhaus	13	Alan Vega	56
Falco	14	Cristina	57
The Cramps	15	The English Beat	58
Glenn Branca	16	Japan	60
Heaven 17	17	Sparks	62
Klaus Nomi	18	Nico	63
Johnny Dee Fury	19	Lords of the New Church	64
David Byrne	20	KaS Product	66
Robert Fripp	21	Thomas Dolby	67
Yellowman	22	Spoons	68
Siouxsie and the Banshees	23	The Cure	70
The Passage	24	Big Country	71
Bush Tetras	25	X	72
Tom Verlaine	26	John Foxx	73
ESG	27	The Fixx	74
Peter Gabriel	28	Howard Devoto	75
Telephone	30	The Blasters	76
Stray Cats	32	The Belle Stars	78
Revillos	33	Joey Ramone	80
Madonna	34	Holly Beth Vincent	81
Defunkt	35	Bad Brains	82
Culture Club	36	James Blood Ulmer	83
Rhys Chatham	38	Fashion	84
Billy Idol	39	Lene Lovich	86
Martha and the Muffins	40	APB	88
Afrika Bambaataa	41	The Style Council	89
Eurythmics	42	Pete Shelley	90
Grandmaster Flash	44	Pylon	91
Nina Hagen	45	Breeding Ground	92
Wall of Voodoo	46	Sting	93
James White and the Blacks	47	Pulsullama	94
Rough Trade	48	Richard Hell	95
Motorhead	50	Joan Jett	96

Lounge Lizards	97
Bernard Szajner	98
Chris Spedding	100
The Birthday Party	101
Duran Duran	102
Taxi Girl	103
Minny Pops	104
John Cale	105
Dead Kennedys	106
King Sunny Ade	107
Public Image Ltd.	108
Julian Cope	110
Jim Carroll	111
Blancmange	112
Rick James	114
David Thomas	115
Bill Nelson	116
Richard Strange	117
Killing Joke	118
Iggy Pop	119
Modern English	120
Orchestral Manoeuvres in the Dark	121
Steel Pulse	122
John Cooper Clarke	124
Nash the Slash	125
Men Without Hats	126
A Flock of Seagulls	127
Laurie Anderson	128
Jayne County	129
Gun Club	130
Shriekback	131
Romeo Void	132
The Stranglers	133
Red Decade	134
U2	135
Leisure Process	136

A SELECTED DISCOGRAPHY 137

ACKNOWLEDGEMENTS

— PARIS —

Martine Houadec   Dominique Mallegni   Francois Ravard   Patrick Mathé   Francis Fottorino   Sylvie Blateyron   Gerard Nguyen   Pierre Satgé   Jonathan Hartman for direction(s)   and Alexi at Mankin.

— LONDON —

Jonathan Hartman (again)   Sian Thomas   Rass Edmunds   Miranda Brown   Ivo Watts   Juliette Joseph   Sheila Sedgwick   Kenny Smith   Chris Rowly   Jackie Moini   Julia Elsdon   Martin Meissonnier.

— NEW YORK —

Mark Beaven   Ruth Polsky   Louise Greife   Peter Wright   Ed Bahlman   Steve Ralbovsky   Donna Rossou   Frank Riley   Tara Dennison   Annie Ammonn   Tracey Nicholas Bledsoe   Michael Zilkha   Anthony Countey   Patricia Samuel   Deloris Hodges   Ed Straight   Monica Lynch   Mitch Pollak   Mike Rosenblatt.

— TORONTO —

Gary Topp   Lisa Elliott   Elliott Lefko   Mark Leach   Shelia Wawanash   Elaine Levene   Karen Gordon   Tim Keele   Randy Sharrard   Llyn Adalist   Larry Macrae   Bobby Gale   Mark Krawczynski   Gerry Young   Gary Cormier   Barbie Shore   Ron Gaskin   Liam Lacey   Chris Allicock   Lorna Richards   Cam Carpenter   Mike Krawczynski   Dave Smeltzer   Bill Johnston   Sandy Bennett-Sayer   Lesley Soldat   Jim Monaco   Jan Crabtree   Dayle Kalnins   Anita Mara Alksnis   Jane Hodgson   Anya Wilson   Joanne Smale   Peter Goddard   Angie Baldassarre   Carl Finkle   Arthur Fogel   Angus Mackay   Record Peddler   Darkroom & Camera   and Sidney & Lila Noble.

INTRODUCTION

One way to look at this book is as situations in which a photographer played it by ear.

By which I mean, yes; it has somethin to do with "rock photographs" you've seen before — and the images in which musicians are framed (and sold out) to a public that buys it and eats it up more or less passively. Still, there are critical differences right from the start.

Peter's choices of subjects here have been determined, I'd say for the most part, by his passionate interest in somebody's music. But the subjects themselves are not standard musicians, in the rock or even a New Wave rock sense. At this point some have become famous, and others might yet if there is any justice: that isn't the point. At the time he was working with them, all these people were working along the frontiers that break down some distinctions that have, in the recent past, tended to settle along rigid lines; between what is art and what's just entertainment, between what's inspired and what is fabricated to "meet a demand." If there's one thing that they have in common, that Peter shares with them, I'd say that it is that they use and refuse to be fixed in the images of an ideal whereby, for example, a market analysis might talk of "profile."

That this posed a dilemma was also, I think, what has piqued Peter's interest in making these photographs. He could not reproduce or appropriate "glamour" (nor could he just invert it) because that was one way to simply betray — one is tempted to say assassinate — what in effect brought him here to each case. To portray his real interest and all of these people, he had to collaborate.

So that makes Peter more than a man with a finger on his camera's pulse. It goes without saying, but I'll say it anyway, that he's an artist. However, the real point to me of this book is that these photographs, and the quotes he's selected, came from and *had* to come out of a dialogue. They do have a real, special quality which I think follows from Peter's combining the strategies, functions and roles of what were in most cases fairly long interviews, and their transcriptions, with those of photography and its development. There is plenty of work in all this, that takes time. There is also the play of invention, conventions, and then some discoveries. It's the range of this process that quickens an interest and makes it decisive; that deepens it with understanding and human respect and that's what, in these photographs, resonates out.

In a sense, they violate certain conventions by which we "see" photographs. They combine what would seem incompatible ends. In some, what we see is all human (which can be quite a shock if we're only expecting publicity's image). In mysterious ways, they can operate on us like our family's snapshots, seeming full of the density of a real memory even if we can't in fact reconstruct it, reduce it to anecdote, get the whole joke. In others we enter the air of ideals — of the good and the beautiful — caught in a moment both guarded and playful, and I think our response to that moment is yearning. We might want to know more about it, about all that surrounds it and brought it to this. But what we are looking at has the finality of a creation and it leaves us frustrated and grateful at once. It's how we recognize not a person but another (certified) personality.

That, face to face with this record, we are able to mix and match up such responses is what, for me, constitutes its real power. It is also quite simply a whole lot of fun. Peter's work might invite speculation — it doesn't force issues/conclusions on anyone. And that's my way of seeing that Peter has principles and — well, say no more. A nudge is as good as a wink if you're not a dead horse because now it's all yours. You can see for yourself if *you* wanna make something of it.

— Sheila Wawanash —

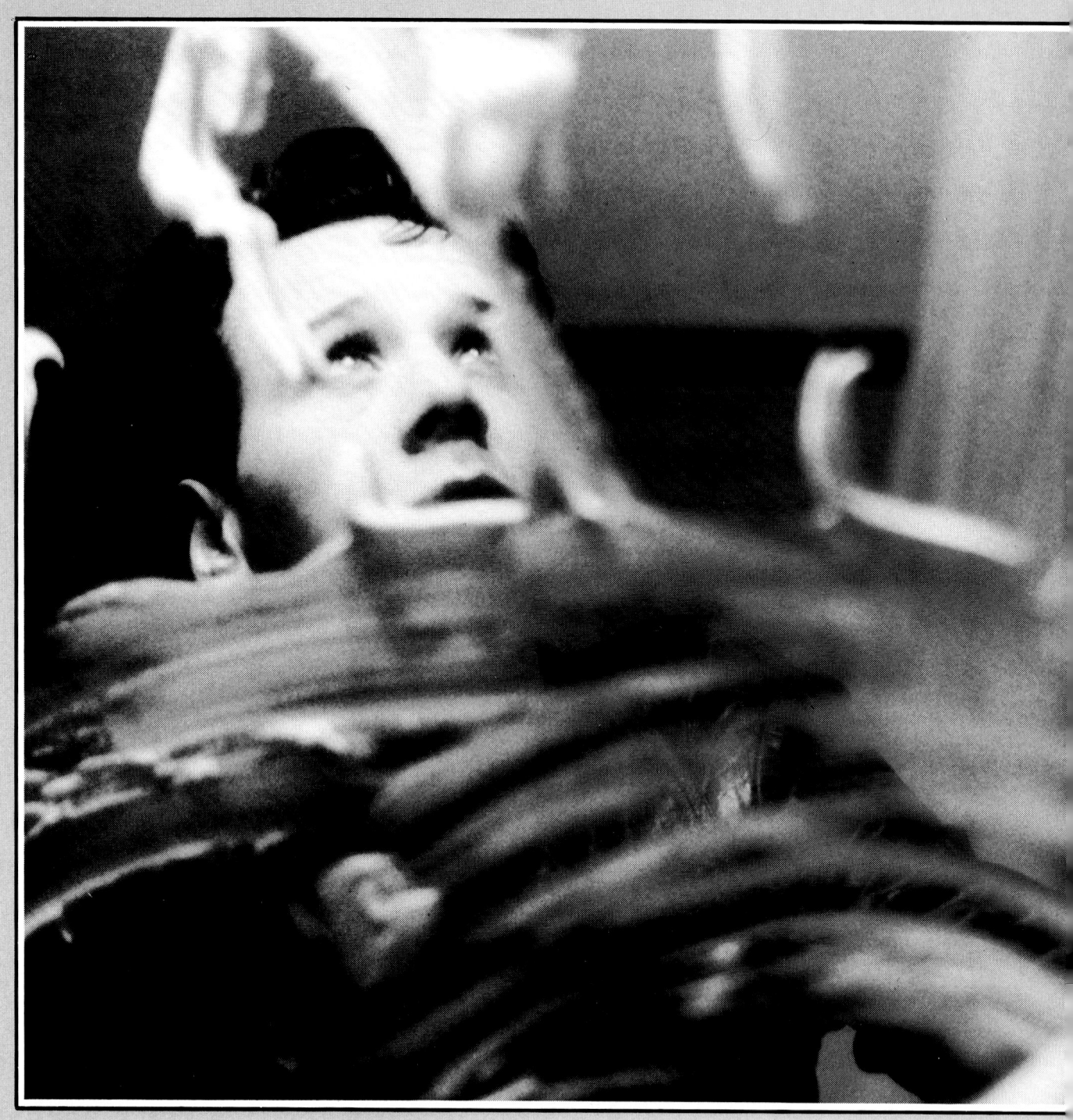

SIMPLE MINDS

"We try to use the voice as an instrument. That's why we don't spend a lot of time trying to make all the words easy to understand. Don't come to us as if we're some kind of big literary figures. I've never learned anything from other songwriters in terms of a verse that will set me up for life. However, I have been touched by the synchronization between the atmosphere of words and the atmosphere of music. People have got to dance to the problems of their time instead of pretending that they don't exist. Celebrate the problems and the confusion. Try to deal with it. Take it for what it is."
— Jim Kerr —

THOMPSON TWINS

— Tom Bailey —   — Joe Leeway —

— Alannah Currie —

"I think we're going to move into the field of futurism. It's not the same sort of futurism that was happening pre-'80s in England with all the clothes — that was cold futurism. What we want to do is start writing songs, like Watching, that are about an extended vision of the future, not just the cold, isolated machine takes over everything kind of thing. Sure, machines probably will be the future, but there will also be the future of music as well. It's already become a lot more technological. But there will always be smelly armpits. There will always be people falling in love. There will always be hatred, too. There are all of these human emotions which are very much a part of the future and we'll never get rid of them. I mean, that's the nice thing — mixing real human banalities with very high-tech visions of where we're going to be thirty years from now. That's the direction we're going to be taking our music in. We're going to put it in a dance format so everyone will be able to dance if they feel like it. Dancing is important. It's universal. It's heart rhythm, everybody's got heart. It's not particularly American, British, or Japanese. It's human. Everyone experiences it."

— Alannah Currie —

"The irony about the Thompson Twins is the three of us should have never been in a group together. On paper it would be ridiculous. We're completely different sorts of people. We're not into the same kind of music, apart from what we do together. Our interests are diametrically opposed. Perhaps that's why our record company was so nervous when they first signed us. They took one look at us and saw three different looking people. I mean, we don't even look the same. Maybe that's part of our attraction."

— Tom Bailey —

FAD GADGET

"I think the music scene in Britain has become extremely wimpy. It's worse now than it ever was before punk. Anyone whose got any kind of self-expression or any valid ideas gets swept aside. The successful people are the ones who churn out the same old disco. It's ridiculous to think the situation we're in in Britain at the moment, with the unemployment and riots, is okay. I'll never be able to figure out how people could carry on singing, 'Let's all dance and have a good time,' when, y'know, life's really not like that. I don't really think pop music reflects society at all. People want escapism. They don't want to think about their problems. The fact of the matter is that nothing is going to change unless everyone starts dealing with real-life issues. I don't know if what I'm doing is challenging anyone's ideas or helping somebody in particular, but at least I'm trying.

"I'm not really a musician. I can't actually sit down and play something. The way I write is by playing two notes over and over again, or playing two chords on a guitar or something. Because I use other musicians, synthesizers, computers, and sequencers to do the manual work, I can decide on what kind of music I want to make from album to album. Say for the next album I wanted to record a rock'n'roll album, a country and western album, or a blues album, I could easily slot into anything. That's why every album I've done has been so radically different. The only thing that's been consistent has been the synthesizers.

"I think you've got to be very careful with the new technology. The problem at the moment is because of drum machines and so on, it's very easy for anyone to sound vaguely musical, but I think it needs to go on from there. Anyone can switch on a drum machine and record it, but I don't think there's very many people using the technology to its full extent at the moment. Everyone is using synthes to re-create brass and string sounds, but nobody's really using it as a tool to invent altogether new sounds."

— Frank Tovey —

BAUHAUS

— From left to right: Daniel Ash, Kevin Haskins, Peter Murphy, David Jay —

"I've never thought about it, but being onstage is like acting, isn't it?"

— Peter Murphy —

FALCO

"I've never understood why most people are accustomed to buying records that are only sung in English. In Germany we don't speak English, but we do listen to a lot of English vocalists. I grew up with it. This is a very natural thing for German people because after the war everything was destroyed. There was no real popular modern culture in the music sector. The Americans and the British had it. That's why English was the first official language in pop. It's taken a good ten years to find German words that fit comfortably into popular music. I mean, that's not exactly correct because, at one time, there used to be a German sound, but it was what you'd call kitch. Y'know, 'Roses in winter, in spring and in summer.' I promise you, it was very unsatisfying to be eighteen years old and copy British and American music.

"I've never felt as if I was a part of the New German Wave. I'm from Vienna. Anyways, ninety percent of it is complete bullshit. I only feel a part to what happened two years ago when everybody began to accept German words in pop. You have to know Vienna from the economical side. We are rather dependent on the Germans, but we always keep a distance from them. They look at us as if we're something exotic. The Austrian dialect is very different from German. If you're an Austrian entertainer and you go to Germany, you have a big credit. It didn't happen so often in the past but these days Austrian performers are becoming very successful in Germany."

The CRAMPS

— Current line-up 1983: Kid Congo, Poison Ivy, Lux Interior, Nick Knox —

"Lux sucks in ectoplasm from another dimension to save the world. Turn blue. Stay sick. Purple knif."

— Lux Interior —

"If you wanna put a picture of us in your book, you've got to take a new one with Kid Congo in the band. It wouldn't be right to rely on the past. Kid Congo is NOW."

— Poison Ivy —

GLENN BRANCA

"Yeah, I think I would consider myself a composer. I don't write songs. I don't write lyrics and melodies. It's not interesting to me anymore. I'm much more interested in the actual sound. I'm not concerned with words. I deal with large masses of sound. It's got more to do with chordal progressions. I don't specifically set out to write the melodies. As far as the resultant tones are concerned, if there's a melody it'll be a combination of a very dense progression of chords. Once I started to hear this incredible depth in the chords that I was sounding, it was totally seductive. I couldn't help but go in that direction.

"When I say that I'm working with mathematics I'm not necessarily working with it in relationship to structure. I'm working with mathematics in relationship to harmony and there's a big difference. For instance, Bach worked with mathematics in relationship to counterpoint. It's something that I'm interested in, but again, I'm not interested in it as much as I am in the field of sound. Any way I get towards creating that field is strictly incidental to the actual sound."

HEAVEN 17

— From left to right: Glenn Gregory, Martyn Ware, Ian Craig Marsh —

"B.E.F. [British Electric Foundation] is a production company that we formed after we split from the original line-up of the Human League. Our main intention was to get away from the idea of the four-man group which has plagued us since the Beatles in the '60s. There are a lot more two- and three-man operations in Britain at the moment. Nowadays it's more of an economic necessity not to have a lot of people on the payroll. As a company we wanted to rid ourselves of the hypocrisy that surrounds most groups who claim to have some kind of street awareness, when, in fact, all they're doing is pumping money into their bank accounts. It's a misconception when they say they're not into money, and that they're artists first and foremost. Rubbish! It's obvious this is as much a career as it is being an accountant. Anyone who denies this is only fooling themselves."

— Martyn Ware —

"Naturally we do enjoy what we're doing but we're not going to sit here and tell you that we don't want to make any money from this. In the past people would ignore this fact. Pink Floyd would sing songs like Money ('it's a drag') and all this kind of crap, when, in fact, they're multi-millionaires. I mean, what the hell are they talking about? They're making a fucking fortune. Believe me, they're all astute businessmen underneath all that hair. It's hypocrisy at its most obvious."

— Ian Craig Marsh —

KLAUS NOMI

"When I left Germany in 1973 I headed straight for New York City. Since then I've been trying to get adjusted, trying to get to know the people and the culture. When I first came to New York it was a real culture shock for me. I explored the clubs and frequented a lot of rock concerts. I didn't go to the opera anymore. I felt very strongly about making it as a rock singer. A friend of mine once told me, 'You can never be a rock singer. Your accent is too German and your voice is too operatic.' That really upset me because I knew I didn't sound like anyone else. I knew I was different.

"The things in life that I enjoy the most are music, theatre, food, and people. When it comes to food I like almost anything really. It has to be prepared very well. I would eat a hot dog on a street corner only as a perversion. I go for hamburgers and greasy french fries very occasionally, but that's like being bad. I enjoy being bad sometimes.

"Sometimes I go out with some friends and they say, 'Let's go down to that restaurant. They have real cheap burgers and they're really good. C'mon, it'll be a lot of fun.' I'll do that and then I'll feel very American and have a coke with it too. But not a diet coke."

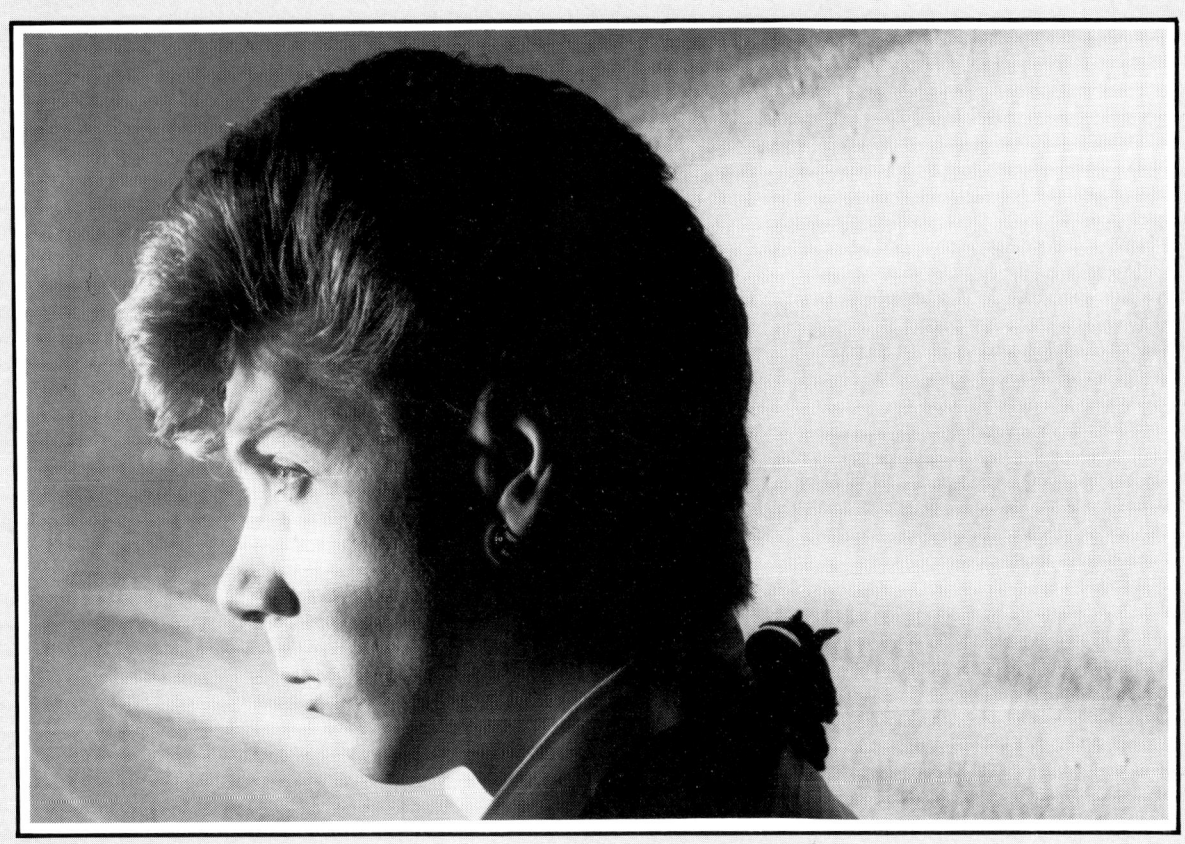

JOHNNY DEE FURY

"The music I play is an extension of what most people usually refer to as rockabilly. This unique American sound was originally pioneered by such '50s greats as Carl Perkins, Elvis Presley, and Gene Vincent. To me, it's what true rock'n'roll is all about. I'm talkin' about the pure essence. It's that SOUND. It's rock with the roll left in it. Man, can it roll. And it's as much a part of the '80s as it was in the '50s. It's simple, passionate music with a monster beat. It's perfect for dancing your heart out to. I love it. I really believe in it, too. I see it move people every time I walk onstage. And that's enough for me."

DAVID BYRNE

"I think since the development of recording studios, and recorded music being an entity on its own, apart from the live performance, there has been more emphasis on the texture of a piece of music, sometimes even more so than the melody. I used to think that's what rock music was all about. Many groups use the same melodies over and over again, but what was important was the overall texture of their singing, music, and rhythm. It all contributed to it. You'd hear a few bars of something and immediately the texture of it said something to you, it communicated the attitude of what the song was about. Without even hearing the lyrics or the melody you could pick up on what the musician was trying to communicate. I began to think we [Talking Heads] should play different textures, not just the ones that are familiar to the average person. A lot of times we'd say, 'Let's do something that has this kind of texture,' rather than going in and thinking, 'Here's the melody and the tempo.' We tried to achieve a certain kind of texture. It didn't really matter what the various parts or melodies were like. For us it's been a successful way of working on material. It gives us a foundation and then, after that, there comes the lyrics and the melodies. We get results that we might not have gotten if we worked along the lines of a tight script."

ROBERT FRIPP

"There's a level on which one's iconic status can be used positively. One has to use this energy in a positive way, but one has to develop an objectivity with the image so one doesn't confuse oneself with it. The Robert Fripp that goes on stage is not the turkey who sits here, he's just an ordinary geezer. In the '60s we said rock'n'roll could change the world. In the '70s we realized it was impossible. I would say in the '80s that, yes, rock'n'roll can change the world, without a shadow of a doubt, but not in the way that we expect."

YELLOWMAN

"You had the reggae king named Bob Marley — he died and left the work so I decided to pick it up and carry on with it — spread reggae as long as possible, yeah. Reggae's a thing that's taking an effect on people all over the world. I want to show them it's one of the best kinds of cultural musics around now. I D.J. in front of big American crowd, not always Jamaican, and they really love it. Reggae has meaning. It have feeling. The thing that surprised me in America is that so many people recognized me. I found out the people love me. It make me feel nice everywhere I go no matter what the crowd is like. It's been an experience. It give me more inspiration to do new and different music. D.J. is an everyday thing for me. I love my fans. For all the D.J.'s who've been making music for so long and never have a hit music I would like for them to have a hit music. There are so many of them who've been toasting before me like Lone Ranger, Big Youth, and Dillinger. They've never had a hit music. I hope they have a hit music and feel alright."

SIOUXSIE and the BANSHEES

"I can remember the time when I kicked someone in the head at one of our gigs. He deserved it. This happened in Coventry, England. Y'know, we've never appreciated the idea of being spat upon. A lot of bozo bands love it but we've always said, 'Don't do it! Stand on your head if you want something different to do.' There was this one guy who wasn't there for the music. It was just an excuse for him to be a total slob. He only wanted to spit and spurt his beer. I was wearing my big black boots and at one point I tried talking to him between songs, telling him to stop. He just ignored me and continued to be an asshole. All of a sudden I kicked him, his mouth caved in and it started bleeding everywhere. After the gig his Mum and his girlfriend got in touch with the concert promoters and tried to threaten us. They said, 'We're gonna fuckin' sue the band!!!'"

— Siouxsie Sioux —

The PASSAGE

— From left to right: Andy Wilson, Dick Witts, Paul Mahoney —

"People robbed of their past seem to be the most fervent picture takers. Photographs are a neat slice of time. Photographs, which cannot themselves explain anything, are inexhaustible invitations to deduction, speculation, and fantasy.
— Dick Witts quoting Susan Sontag, on photography, 1977 —

BUSH TETRAS

— Cynthia Sley — — Bobbie Alberston — — Donnie Christensen — — Pat Place —

"In New York there's this expression that's pretty popular at the moment — 'It's so weird.' I mean, EVERYBODY says, 'It's so weird.' It's such a truism, y'know. Everything is so weird. This week my husband's sister is almost dying. They're going to operate on her tomorrow. His best friend just went in the hospital for his pancreas and almost died. Three friends of my prarents just died. I mean, everybody's dying in February. It's as if everything's happening at once! It is weird. I mean, the chain of events are weird. And in New York it's really intense. Everything happens really fast.

"When we came to play Toronto it was weird. We came in and sensed this bad vibe. This time it was...I...I...I mean, it was SO weird. See what I mean? You just use it all the time. We feel like it just says it all. You pull into a place, you've got a really positive attitude about what you're doing and you just end up getting fucked over, y'know? I mean, nobody wants to come to the club. All these people called, they got all this response but nobody came! It doesn't make any sense! It's just weird. The guy spitting in your face. That's weird. And then saying goodbye to you. That's weird. Y'know, it's jut like life can be very weird. In music you have to deal with all these different people all the time. Half of them are involved with the Mafia anyways. It's like you're constantly on this push and pull system. You have to be exposed to all of it but you also have to deal with it. I think we deal with it pretty well. I mean, we could give up and not deal with it but, y'know, it's like we've accepted the fact that things are WEIRD."

— Cynthia Sley —

TOM VERLAINE

"When I come across an idea for a song I usually have to get some kind of a feeling from it. If I don't get a feeling from it I'll abandon it right away. Now, whether that feeling is being elated or sad, at least it's okay to feel something. I mean, take a look at rock'n'roll, certainly half of it is a new kind of muzak. Originally muzak was invented to soothe the nerves and the environment, whereas the rock muzak of today doesn't necessarily set out to soothe one's nerves at all. It's a mild stimulant for the nerves 'coz the beats are up and the drums pound away. It increases the heartbeat and maybe that's why it makes people feel stimulated when they're driving their cars. The bands and the sounds are so canned, unindividual, and formulized that it's almost as if it's become a new kind of background music for the '80s. Mild stimulant rather than mild sedative. If I go to a doctor's office the muzak doesn't do a thing for me. They say it subliminally relaxes you but I would just as soon not hear it. I think it's irritating. When I was last on tour I spent most of my time listening to country and western stations. In some C & W songs there's still an attempt at communicating feeling. I guess it's unfair for me to say that rock groups don't have any feeling. I suppose they think they're doing something important, although I don't really know. I just don't know anymore."

ESG

— From left to right: Marie Scroggins, Tito Libran, Renee, Deborah and Valerie Scroggins —

"We want to be different. We don't wanna sound like anybody else. We play less instruments. We don't have to go in for all these heavy synthesizers. Why? It's too complicated. We want to keep it simple and basic. The bass guitar is our lead instrument. We lean on a lot of heavy bass for a funk type of sound but other bands usually focus on the guitar, synthesizer, and the organ. Funk to me is like heavy bass, lots of rhyhm. It's music you can get into, you can feel it. That's what real funk is all about. You can feel it vibrating through your body. Drums play a big part but the main emphasis is on the bass guitar."

— Deborah Scroggins —

"There's a lot of emptiness in the Bronx, but there's also a lot of fullness, in the people I mean. Sometimes Manhatten can be very cold. I like the Bronx for the vibrations I get from it. It really helps us with our music. There's so much stuff happening in the Bronx. There's good and there's bad. Maybe that's why we tend to keep the music so simple. The Bronx is rough. It really is. Because it's so rough it made us wanna do somethin' positive with our lives. There were a lot of rotten things going on where we live. Instead of us hanging out and getting into this stuff, my mother bought us instruments and we did somethin' creative instead of hangin' out on the streets."

— Renee Scroggins —

PETER GABRIEL

"Unlike some of the others of my generation of so-called progressives, I'm not ashamed of my past. Your past is part of who you are, but because you don't perform or want to make a certain kind of music anymore doesn't mean that you disown any connection with it. I just found myself fascinated with different things in the last few years, especially rhythm. I think I first really discovered it when I wrote the song Biko. I found myself listening to one rhythm pattern for hours and feeling completely satisfied.

"I'm not pretending that I understand African or any other kind of so-called primitive music that stresses rhythm. That kind of thing would take twenty years of training and even then you might not really understand it, but it fascinates me anyway, so I pursue it in my own clumsy way."

TELEPHONE

— Corinne Marienneau —

— Richard Kolinka —

— Louis Bertignac —   — Jean-Louis Aubert —

"We were probably the first French pop group to have success in our own country. Before us there was no other in France. When we first started, our shows were very powerful and energetic. I think people were finally ready for French pop music because in the past all there were were MOR singers and a lot of English and American music. The young people needed someone to look up to, someone to lead them. Everybody needs a culture or a leader they can imitate or follow. The kids needed someone who was just like them. Telephone were just like them. I mean, now we might be getting some money and things like that, but even now people think we're just like them. When they meet us on the street or in a restaurant they treat us as if we're their friends. They usually come up to me and say, 'Oh yeah, I know you. You know I'm just like you.' I know they're like me. We respect the same sort of things in life."

— Louis Bertignac —

"When you're eighteen years of age you begin to see, very clearly, the bad aspects of everyday life. You begin to see the things you don't want. But when you begin to live by yourself, you begin to see that it's not that easy. You start telling yourself, 'Maybe I'm doing the things I never said I would do.' I would like to bring more courage to people and share more but, y'know, I don't throw the stone to people like I used to. I know it's difficult, even with money — with everything. Before I used to think the world existed with a lot of horrible people and now I'm terrified to see everything is very human and I am human too. So I can recognize part of myself in the mirror of the words. Now I just say it's humanity."

— Jean-Louis Aubert —

STRAY CATS

— From left to right: Slim Jim Phantom, Brian Setzer, Lee Rocker —

"We don't feel as if we're part of a movement. We don't really have anything in common with your usual rockabilly groups. All these guys say, 'Hey, rockabilly rebels,' and they hang out the Confederate flag. We were always different because we never... Well, first of all, we never did that... hung up on all that nonsense and, um, we always played, y'know, a couple of blues tunes to break things up. We'd also play some rockers, rockabillies and American roots music. The rest of these groups thought they were rockabilly rebels and that's why they'd only play rockabilly songs, nothin' more. Everyone is always trying to corner you, so why try to corner yourself?

"Our audiences are really varied. In England we get rockabillies, Teds, and punks. A lot of punk girls come to see us and I haven't been able to figure out why. We also get what you would call normal kids. That's what it's like in England — it's a real mix. In France I have to say it's exclusively rockers. They've definitely got their rocker thing happening."

— Slim Jim Phantom —

REVILLOS

— From left to right clockwise: Vince Spik, Fay Fife, Kid Krupa, Eugene Reynolds —

"That's another thing... PSYCHEDELIC!!! Bloody hell! We got into psychedelia when the Where's The Boy For Me single came out. Now we're doing a song called Superville. The lyrics and the accompanying music are really psychedelic but nobody in the group likes to make mention of that. If you want to put it that way, yes, I guess we are a psychedelic group as much as we're anything else because we're a distorted vision of what goes on in real life. When all of these new bands came along and said, 'We're into psychedelia. Isn't it fantastic?', it really left me cold. They were the same people who were probably into punk, mod, and the futurist fads as well. It all boils down to fashion, and fashion bores us to tears. We would rather remain in left field and continue to move on instead of being picked up and dropped like a dead skunk.

"The people that usually go mental over us are quite crazy as it is. They can see into what we're doing and they take what they want out of that. Sometimes they have their own interpretations of what the Revillos are about which are slightly different from how we see ourselves but I find it all very interesting. Sometimes you get these really fanatical fans following the band on the road. We've got this one fan in particular who comes to our gigs dressed in silver scuba suits, pink propeller boots, and silver hair with jet packs on his back. He dresses up just like Scuba Boy. He looks like he just stepped out of an outer space movie. He never really says much. He usually says 'hello' and then he walks away."

— Fay Fife —

MADONNA

"I'm a dancer. I know what it's like to watch things and get bored very easily. That's why I wanted to combine dancing, y'know, just like on 'Solid Gold' [an American T.V. rock show]. Everybody watches that. They listen to the music and they watch people dance. That's what they enjoy. I wanted to combine that with the old Motown stuff where there are dancers in the back doing all those hand movements and singing background vocals with much more concentration on dance. I wanted to work out a scenario to every song. That's what I'm doing right now. I'm building up my repertoire. I'm singing live to taped music and using dancers. There's no live band accompanying me. Maybe if I played to some hardcore AC/DC fans they probably wouldn't be into it, but so far everyone's really liked it.

"Dancing is sexually provocative. It's moving to music only you're by yourself. It's masturbatory. You're just moving your body to music. It's like sex. It feels that good to me. I think it feels that good to other people as well. Nowadays people don't dance with each other, they just DANCE!!! It's like getting into yourself, moving your body all around and stuff. When you're on the dance floor you can feel the bass and the percussion. It's very primitive and sexual. It's a wonderful way to express yourself. Am I beating around the bush? No? I mean, it's hard to be really precise about these matters (giggle). Dancing and music and sex — they're all the same thing. It comes from your soul ultimately. To express yourself deep down inside is important. If you didn't you'd be just like a dead person."

DEFUNKT

"I have a concept of life in my music which is about freedom, survival, and rebellion from the restrictions of the past. It's about young people, tradition, and authenticity. These feelings are expressed in the form of high energy, high emotional content, and energetic visual concepts. All these things comprise the idea of what I wanted in the band. The funk things we do are very groovy because they're African and polyrhythmic. I think that's what throws a lot of people off. They think it's jazz. In Defunkt every musician plays an individual rhythm. It's very polyrhythmic. That's what makes it roll around like a wheel. Once that groove starts it's as if it's a freight train or somethin'. It's multi-layered. It can push on and on indefinitely. The style and attitude of our music is like another step of maturity for a rock'n'roll audience. Style is finesse. It's havin' a strong presence, a good audience, and a lot of honesty."

— Joe Bowie —

CULTURE CLUB

— Boy George —

— Roy Hay  —   — Jon Moss  —   —Michael Craig—

"Culture Club music sexual? Not at all! That's one of the things I never wanted to be. In England there was a review of one of our concerts that said, 'It was as if Culture Club invited us along to celebrate their success.' That's what I want. I want people to celebrate. Dress up for the evening. It doesn't matter if they never dress up again. If they stick on dreadlocks and stick a hat on I don't care. I want people to enjoy themselves for the right reasons, not for the wrong reasons. I don't want people committed to an ideal 'coz ideals go out the window after a while. Things aren't black and white to me. I could say something to you now and tomorrow something could happen that would make me change my mind. What about the people who believe in God all their lives and then suddenly one of their kids dies? Next thing you know they stop believing in God. If you believe in something for the wrong reason then it's going to let you down sooner or later. You asked me what's my definition of beauty? I mean, some people are happy being fat, and yet, they get ridiculed for it. I think if someone's happy being fat that's fabulous. That's why I like Helen [C. Club's backup vocalist]. She's odd. I'm odd. I don't think I'm sexy at all."

— Boy George —

"After the Blitz movement things had to start warming up. I thought spiritualism had to come about, not actual 'spiritualism,' but people becoming more aware of abstract ideas and wanting more than just staying out all night and getting drunk. It had something to do with becoming more aware of what was going on around you. In other words becoming a day person instead of an all-night person, which is what we've done while we've been here in New York. We haven't gone nightclubbing. We want to see New York in the daylight. In England the nightclub thing happened for a good two years. People stayed out all night long. They still do it to some extent. Do you understand what I'm saying? London is just like New York. There's so many different cultures and nationalities — Italians, Chinese people, Jews, Greeks, Indian people, Pakistanis. Culture is very important. It seemed to be such a fitting word. It is the word for 1983."

— Jon Moss —

RHYS CHATHAM

"In the '50s, composition was a vital field with surrealism, electronic music and what was referred to as 'processed' or 'phased' music by Steve Reich and Phillip Glass. The idea of electronic music in the '50s was about expanding a vocabulary and opening up a limitless palette of sound. John Cage once said that any sound can follow any sound. If you take that to its logical conclusion you can do anything you want musically. Now that we know we can do anything we desire, the question is what exactly do we want to do? What I foresee happening now, and in the near future, is combining existing sounds in new ways. A synthesis of world music. In the '50s a classical composer didn't know anything about jazz or rock. Jazzers didn't even know about classical. Now a jazz artist like Anthony Braxton knows everything there is to know about Stockhausen. Braxton even works with a classical composer these days. I mean, it's getting incredibly confused, mixed up, and weird. And the weirder its gets the better I like it."

BILLY IDOL

"I needed to leave England for New York, to meet new people so my mind wouldn't turn blank. There's this idea that by coming to America and playing to ordinary people, which is the biggest proletariat nation in the world, apart from Russia, coming here is bad vibes for some British people, like you've sold out. In fact, what you're doing is selling in. There are so many people who are doing normal jobs. They're coalmining, they're building fucking cars, they're on horrible treadmill existences. So if people think I'm a cunt for going to America, they're wankers. I've actually come over to play where punk rock should be. This is where most of the work force of the world is anyways. I did my bit for England — six years. And they decided they wanted Spandau Ballet. I've come here to get extra energy, have more fun, and play to a lot of people who've never seen me before. Listen to what's being played on the radio at the moment. At least we can hope to dent it a bit so that we can get some new people in, whoever they are."

MARTHA and the MUFFINS

— From left to right: Jocelyne Lanois, Mark Gane, Martha Johnson, Nick Kent —

"You've got to understand the music industry wants stars and they want people to believe that every morning I wake up there's a limousine that takes me to a trendy restaurant where I dine on exotic seafood. But that's not the case at all. We're middle class. We all come from the suburbs. I make no apology for that. I think we're representing our backgrounds. To me that is being honest and if people don't like that type of honesty, that's fine. We don't particularly want to be rock stars anyway."

— Mark Gane —

"Someone once asked me if I would like to be interviewed for an article about women in rock, and so, naturally, I asked them if it was something like doing an article about dogs in showbusiness."

— Martha Johnson —

AFRIKA BAMBAATAA

"Rap originated in the Bronx around 1970 with a Jamaican fellow named Cool D. J. Herc. He took this form of music and approached it much in the same way the Jamaicans did — toasting over instrumental dubs and echoes. The only difference was that he used the percussion breaks, drums and bass and anything else that sounded funky, and kept it going back and forth. He'd rap over it, make up words on the spot and make people scream. This type of music was called 'Hip Hop'. Herc never called it by that name. Years later other rappers started sayin', 'To the hip hop you don't stop!' He was the first, then myself and then Grandmaster Flash. We were the only three who were doing this type of music in the Bronx [circa '75-'77].

"It was popular in the Black and Hispanic communities. Everyone got tired of hearing disco and doin' the hustle. Disco was more boom, boom, boom, y'know, Donna Summer stuff. Very plastic. Our music was more funky. Disco has a tempo that's more high energy whereas funk has a heavier bass bottom and heavier percussion breaks. Rap started to get really popular during 1979 when the Fat Back Band recorded the very first rap record King Tim the III. It didn't go over too well. After that came the Sugarhill Gang and they did more of a street-type rap song called Rapper's Delight, and that really put rap on the map.

"Suddenly rap music started fading away. People weren't buying that many records. One day I said to myself, 'We've got to come up with a different style of rapping, somethin' that would catch on with everybody, not just Blacks and Hispanics but with whites, punk rockers and people from other cultures — Chinese, French, gays and straights.' So we looked at the groups who were really making different types of new music for the future and that's when we decided to concentrate on the German electronic group Kraftwerk. They'd been involved in electronic music for years but nobody ever paid that much attention to the amazing dance rhythms in their music. I thought it would be interesting to take Trans Europe Express and one of their recent songs, Numbers, and mix them to a couple of our hip hop type break records like Super Sporm by Captain Sky and The Mexican by Babe Ruth, y'know, something like a Clint Eastwood spaghetti western movie, and mix 'em all together. We were only trying to please the hip hoppers and the punk rockers but then it suddenly took off in the discos and then even Chinese people started gettin' off on it. Radio picked up on it too. We called the record Planet Rock, and in a way it really lived up to its title. England, France and Germany started gettin' hot on it. We couldn't believe it."

EURYTHMICS

— Annie Lennox —

— Dave Stewart —

"The first step towards perfecting Eurythmics was by getting away from the usual format where you have five members in a group. They're the ones who usually have their pictures taken together, travel in limousines and so on. Suddenly you find yourself in the position of working with a group of musicians whether the musical ideas are progressing or not. And that's exactly what happened with the Tourists at a very early stage. Dave and I never want to be in that situation again. I think now, more than ever, we want to follow our own creative bent. Obviously we want to tour, but that can take up a great deal of time. If there were thirty-six hours to each day, we'd be very happy. We tend to fill up our days with a helluva lot of activity. We want to try and do other things besides music. Film work seems to be a number one priority at the moment. However, I do think it's important for us to experiment with new sounds. We have to change from album to album, especially when it comes to style. Eurythmics are two individuals working together. We want control over what we produce. I'm sorry, but we won't let anybody interfere with our music, otherwise the end product could turn into a diluted version of the original idea, which is what happened with the Tourists really."

— Annie Lennox —

"I've started using a computer to mix the live sound during our recent performances instead of just adhering to the standard guitar, bass and drum routine. I play guitar, Mickey Gallagher plays keys and synthes, and Clem Burke plays the drums. We don't have a bassist. The only actual sounds that you hear come from Mickey and myself. The computer has leads going into Mickey's synthes on the other side of the stage, and if I punch a sequence into it, whenever he plays a chord I'll adjust what he's playing according to the time/tone that I've already set into the computer. I've also got the computer linked up to other synthes, space echoes and things. I'm basically mixing all the sounds through my amp directly into the audience. What happened in the '70s was that everyone played their instruments to a set volume and they left it up to the soundman at the back of the venue to adjust the sound levels. In a way, that was pointless because everybody played without knowing whether the lead guitar was coming out loud enough or not. In effect, the musicians played away and the audience heard the soundman's idea of what the song should sound like. That's the neat thing about my little set-up. For example, I can adjust the level of the keyboards from where I'm playing onstage. It's just a matter of having more direct control over the sounds when we're trying to reproduce our music in a live situation."

— Dave Stewart —

GRANDMASTER FLASH

"I used to dream about certain things as far as mixing records was concerned. That's when I came up with the 'Quick Mix.' I extended the short climatic parts of records as long as I wanted. That's what the problem was when I used to match the other jocks. If they would've been aware of keeping the high points going from the lowest possible points, the paying customers would enjoy the parties a lot more. Some people don't wanna hear the entire record. There's just one part of the record they enjoy. That's what I specialize in — taking the best part of a record, even if it's the shortest part, and mixing it. But you have to be fast! You have to know when to stop the record, when to cue it. For a long time I was criticized for doin' it 'coz nobody else was doin' it. When I started, my sound system was nuthin'. I grew up underprivileged so I didn't have the best of mixers. All I had going for me was a technique.

"The first rapper who complimented my spinning was Keith Wiggins, better known as 'Cowboy.' He was like a 'Simon Says' type of rapper. He'd say stuff like, 'Throw your hands in the air. Wave 'em like you just don't care! If you like the sounds that are goin' down, somebody say "Oh, yeah."' And he'd get a tremendous 'OH YEAH' back, so I knew this guy could help me. When I'd spin the records, some of the people who knew their music would say, 'Well God, he's taken the best part of this song and it sounds pretty good.' The majority of the crowd would turn around and say, 'What is this guy doing?' Before I knew it about three-quarters of the crowd would be watchin' me. Very few people would be dancin'! I can't say they got me angry, but I used to say, 'God, what can I do to get these people to party?' I mean, that's what my objective is — to keep them dancing. It wasn't supposed to be like a school session or anything."

NINA HAGEN

"The reason I didn't do an LP for such a long time was because of Glotzer, my former management, and CBS. They were fighting over some stupid contract. I was sitting there with these wonderful ideas and wonderful musicians and Glotzer would always go to CBS and tell them I wasn't ready, I was pregnant. I would have loved to have had it when I was pregnant, it would have been the holiest record in the whole wide world.

"I don't know. CBS is a stupid Babylon company (giggle). I feel very close to God. I already asked Steve Strange if he was the new messiah."

WALL of VOODOO

—From left to right: Mark Moreland, Stanard Ridgway, Joe Nanini, Bill Noland, Chas T. Gray—

Ridgway: "We're going to be appearing on the 'Dick Clark Show.' Why not? We're getting paid for it, right? I have a new scenario I've been trying to sell to this guy who does these comedy skits for television in Los Angeles. It's my version of 'American Bandstand.' I call it 'Armenian Handstand.' You have Dick Clarkagean as the host, right?, and the usual 'American Bandstand' trip with the kind of tubular set-up with the nautical look or whatever it is. You'd have two forty-foot-high meat kabobs spinning on either side of him. Meanwhile, you'd have all these kids standing out in front of the stage and Dick would be standing behind this podium. The final touch would be, maybe this is something only peculiar to Los Angeles, but you would have groups of five to six Armenian men hanging about, loitering..."

Nanini: "...And making remarks about women's tits as they walked by. 'Hey baby, I like your tits!'"

Ridgway: "Yeah, I think maybe I'll tell Dick about that on the show. He has to have a Lavier microphone though, a long one. A long Dowell microphone or we won't do it."

JAMES WHITE and the BLACKS

"I believe in intensity within music. I can't stand blandness. Most of the new music of today is so boring. People who are considered to be New Wave are really quite bland. Most people try to make songs that sound really pleasant. I don't believe in being pleasant at all. I'm not out to please anyone. I'm not out to make anyone hate it either. It isn't in my nature to make something people are going to enjoy. It's got something to do with making them feel an emotion. Most people don't even know what real emotions and feelings are anyways. They're so, especially in this country, living in their own safe world. What I want to do is shatter their world and make them aware of what pain is. The main emotion to be expressed in any kind of art, to me it all comes from pain of some sort. Happiness and things like that are boring as far as I'm concerned. There's nothing more boring than listening to happy music. I mean, that's like really BLAH! It's nothing. It's just like oatmeal for the ears. It's tapioca pudding.

"I'm a very violent person inside but I choose to express it in my music rather than smashing windows. I used to do things like that. When I first came to New York I used to walk down the street, holding a glass I'd just stolen from some club, and I'd smash it on the sidewalk. I'd get into fights but nothing too spectacular. In the early days of the Contortions I used to have a very violent stage act. I'd go into the audience and start attacking people. At that time everybody in New York had this ridiculously cool attitude — 'I've seen everything. You can't shock me. I'm too cool.' I just wanted to prove to them they weren't. I went out and did something that forced them to respond."

— James White —

ROUGH TRADE

—Carol Pope—

— Kevan Staples and girlfriend Marilyn Kiewiet —

"We originally began in 1968 but it took until 1980 before anyone dared to put out a record of ours. We attempt to break down barriers, cross borderlines. The public were the first ones to accept us. Unfortunately, we became the blacksheep of the Canadian recording industry. Our early songs were much more explicit than they are now. I can give you a few titles of songs from 1973: Lipstick on my Dipstick and Auto Erotic Love, the latter focusing on the subject of masturbation. The song really went over well live. We also did a whole revue on stage entitled Restless Underwear with the New York transvestite 'Divine'.

"Also, who would want to put out a record with the kind of songs we were doing? I never swear in my lyrics, but they were still too explicit. It's not that easy to categorize me as a certain kind of singer. People like to be able to compare you with others — 'Oh, she's like Janis Joplin,' but they couldn't do that with me. It's a typical Canadian tendency to fail to recognize their creative artists. They have to become famous in another country before they can be recognized in their own. Now that we've had a bit of success, people try to put us down because they have this incredible inferiority complex about being Canadians."
— Carole Pope —

"Canada is such a vast country — it takes so long for us to get from one end to another. The important thing is to break down these distances. The only way to do that is with the aid of communication systems and how they work. Obviously video, the telephone, and the computer play an integral role. Carole and I might perform in Germany without ever leaving Toronto by doing a satellite broadcast. Ideas and music will become universal and less 'Billboard Chart' oriented, sort of more along the lines of how books are. You can buy them anywhere in the world and sometimes they're translated into several different languages. I'd like to take part in something similar, whereby you could conceivably write songs with people anywhere in the world who wanted to be accessed without having to go there. If I wanted to phone and work with them why should it be such a big deal that we had to be introduced to each other or had to go and meet in one spot of the world? Why should it be difficult for a David Byrne and myself to get together? Because we don't know each other? When each one of us has something to offer for the other? It would be great to master a worldwide pool of information to feed off of. Soon people will be able to be anywhere in the world, at any time, without actually having to go there."
— Kevan Staples —

MOTORHEAD

— Lemmy Kilmister —   — Philthy "Animal" Taylor —

Animal: "Sometimes plane rides can be really enjoyable. When we come over there's a whole road crew as well as the band — you're talkin' about twelve or fourteen people all shit-faced out of their minds for eight hours on an airplane. Most people are doing the same thing anyway. They wanna kill time so they get a wee drunk and have a good time. You end up hanging out in the aisles rapping to the stewardesses."

Lemmy: "We almost got thrown off a plane after we'd been in jail in Finland though."

Animal: "Oh yeah, we got busted in Finland and spent three days in jail for thrashing some hired equipment and making what was a caravan turn into a boat. The bloody thing ended up in the middle of the lake. I think somebody let the brake off or something. Something terrible happened. It sort of just rolled down the hill into the water, didn't it Lem?"

Lemmy: "It was an accident, yeah. We were going through customs and we got arrested and thrown in jail for three days. When we got out we were escorted back to the plane, Scandinavian Airlines I believe. We went crazy because we hadn't had a drink for three days. As soon as we got on the plane we drank everything in sight. ARRRGH!!! We ran all over the plane laughing uproariously."

Animal: "Suddenly this Scandinavian captain walked back to our seats and said, 'Any more of zis trouble and we'll radio ze police and you vill be arrested when you land in Denmark.'
We had to stop over in Copenhagen on our way back home to London. When we got there we had about an hour to kill in between plane rides. We ended up drinking elephant beer and so naturally we got even more pissed. Obviously the word must have got around to the captain on the next plane because just before the flight was ready to take off he came back and said, 'Now I'd just like to warn you guys that I've heard about you. If there's any noise or any trouble I'll guarantee you'll be arrested when we hit London.' As soon as he fucked off we just carried on. We weren't really annoying anybody. We were just being a bit loud, boisterous, and drunk. I mean, we weren't exactly gobbing on the passengers or spilling drinks."

Lemmy: "I think we annoyed that woman on the first plane when Eddy [Motorhead's ex-guitarist] accidentally poured his drink down her back. That was what started the whole thing wasn't it? 'Coz he was leaning over his seat going, 'Yarrgh!!...oh sorry mate.' Ice cubes all down her back. It was a nasty scene. I don't think he really meant to do it. I mean, you can usually tell when people are sincere but I think Eddy blew it when he started breaking out in a fit of laughter."

BOW WOW WOW

— Annabella Lwin —

— Leroy Gorman —

52

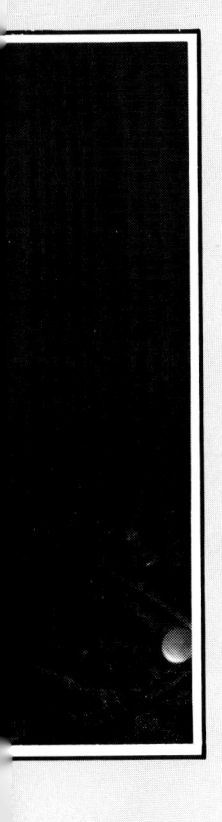

—Matthew Ashman—
—Dave Barbarossa—

"The difference between what we're doing now as opposed to what we were doing when we first started out, is that now we're more direct, more succinct, but just as hedonistic. We've always felt as if we've had hedonistic roots, whether it was for sex or pure play. I'd call it a mix of optimism, enthusiasm, liveliness, and a search for solutions to problems. It's just human excitement, y'know? I don't mean shouting and having a good time, I mean real excitement.

"We just finished doing this film with Sir John Gielgud. It's called 'Scandelous' and it looks like a real laugh! At one point Gielgud gets all leathered up for the part. He wears a leather motorcycle cap. He even has 'Bow Wow Wow' written on the back of his leather jacket. I'm not too sure if he had a mohawk because he wore a hat when I saw him. It's a crazy film though. Lots of people running all over the place. Gielgud plays opposite this Australian actress, Pamela Stephenson. He plays the part of an outrageous old school-type of a con man and Pamela portrays the part of his niece. He tries to teach her the tricks of the trade. They set up this guy portrayed by Robert Hayes, y'know, the guy who starred in 'Airplane'? They set him up for a murder rap so he's determined to chase them around, trying to find them while they're conning other people. At one point Gielgud says to one of the supporting characters, 'I'll meet you at the Bow Wow Wow gig tonight.' Naturally there's all these strange characters who turn up, y'know, Mohicans with little cameras in their hair taking pictures."

— Leroy Gorman —

GABI DELGADO

"D.A.F. [Deutsch Amerikanische Freundschaft] was the kind of band that had a very severe, minimalistic concept in music. We were a two-piece who only sung in German. We restricted ourselves by using electronics, acoustic drums and vocals. It was concentrated power, the more minimal the better. Eventually, after three albums, we realized that we had reached our limits. The question was, 'Are we going to continue and maybe repeat the whole thing again, or should we stop and do something completely new?' D.A.F. was a band that never wanted to look back. I'm still good friends with Robert Görl [the D.A.F. drummer], but when you work with someone for five years you get into a routine of exchanging ideas. Suddenly you discover that you're saying the same thing you said two albums previously. For me it's a very normal thing. I wish a lot of bands would break up after two or three albums.

"I was originally born in Spain. I lived there for eight years before I moved to Germany. Now I'm much more interested in a Spanish/Latin approach to music. After D.A.F. folded I went on a working holiday to Spain and South America. To my surprise, I discovered there was a crossover of different musical styles but no real South American sound. South American music is made up from parts of African music, Spanish music, and Indian music. It's a real melting pot of styles.

"I found I was very interested in Spanish and English as languages as opposed to German. The way you sing in Spanish and English is completely different. Suddenly you're given a lot of freedom, I suppose mainly because of the syllables. When singing in Spanish you can stretch syllables and even leave some of them out. You can enunciate them very quickly. Suddenly everything became easier for me, just by using Spanish, thinking in Spanish, and writing the lyrics in Spanish. If you want to you can try rapping in Spanish and it will sound very good, whereas, in German, you need to have a fixed idea. I mean, German is a very precise language."

PSYCHEDELIC FURS

"I don't get impressed by people who sell a few records and then start feeling as if they're something special. It's ridiculous. There will be another band that will come along. There will always be another band. That was the only good thing about the whole punk movement because it said, 'You too can get up on stage and do this. You can make your own music.' That's what probably prompted us to get off our asses. I mean, the pop star attitude is so pompous. I don't see it as being more important than any other job really.

"I used to have heroes, but not anymore. Heroes are people who do things you feel you can't do yourself. I don't feel that unimportant anymore. Now I can do what I want to. People are so often disillusioned by heroes. They are never what you want them to be. When the end of the day comes around you should look inside yourself for gods and idols."

— Richard Butler —

ALAN VEGA

— Suicide 1978: Martin Rev, Alan Vega —   — Alan Vega 1983 —

"If the government isn't going to help you then you have to let loose in some way. Anything's cool, but the minute you stop an automobile from moving... Let's face it, we're all cowboys. The automobile and the gun. It's the heavy trip. It's a substitution for the old horse-opera trip that happened in the nineteenth century. It's an ego-sexual thing. A lot of guys feel stronger if they have a gun. What does it represent? A sexual impotency kind of trip? Do they feel more manly or something? If they get into their big cars, if they get into their big tank they feel — 'HEY, WOW, NOW!' If they're just walking around the streets like everybody else they won't feel that hot. That's what it's a substitute for. It's the drive."

CRISTINA

"There are certain famous pop stars who have dinner with people I don't much care for, ones who drink champagne every night and take a lot of coke, and their lyrics are surprisingly 'streetwise.' There's a real urban issue right now which I feel very strongly about. In the sixties, everybody was rebelling and political idealism was in. In the seventies, people tried to have life-style idealisms such as feminism, free sex and drugs. They discovered that free sex de-sexualized sex and women could sleep with a man on the first night and not be called a whore. Now in the eighties people don't have any political idealism whatsoever. The woman of the eighties isn't just searching for love or for some spiritual happiness. Eveything's wrapped up in self-image and I suppose there's a slightly sado-masochistic theme to a lot of my songs which isn't just whips and chains.

"One time a critic quoted me when I said, 'And once I had a lover, once I had a profession, and once I laughed at nothing and they called it a depression.' He wrote, 'It almost leads me to think that the rich are even more neurotic and unhappy than the rest of us.' Well, this is not at all what I meant. I think all women can relate to that. The problem with media hype and all of this depersonalizing and thinking of oneself as a commodity in the eighties is that both men and women have to deal with it now. A girl, whether she reads Cosmopolitan or The New York Times, is either going to meet the man of her dreams, get married and be a good mother and/or have a career. Sometimes more and more women, it doesn't matter what class we're in, what economic background we come from, or what our aspirations are, like to assume we'll meet up with Mr. Right.

"Let's say you're working in the cosmetics counter at Bloomingdale's. That's no girl's idea of a career anymore! Girls want a profession instead of a job. Everything's so hyped to the point that people are overcome by a real feeling of inadequacy if they don't rate. And I don't see that as a class issue in any way."

The ENGLISH BEAT

— Saxa (with original band) —   — Dave Wakeling —   — Everett Morton —
— David Steel —

— Dave Blockhead —   — Ranking Roger —   — Andy Cox —

"We're trying to get a hard, powerful sound but we don't want to sound heavy metal. And then there's melody, but that doesn't mean we want to sound like Perry Como! Special Beat Service is the first album of ours that's received nothing but good reviews. Our previous two, especially the second, got really slagged off when they were originally released. Now they're saying what a classic album Wha'ppen? was. Whereas this one is considered to be on the ball. I always think critical acclaim in England is like a consolation prize for not selling any records. We used to get into the number one and two spots in the singles charts. Now we're lucky if we get into the 20s or 30s. The only thing that frightens me is this album has already sold twice as many as the first two put together in America — which could mean we're finished artistically.

"What if the new album stiffed? What if everybody thought it was a load of pure shit? Those were just a few of the thoughts that raced around my head before the album was initially released. You used to think your fans cared about you and crap like that, but really, they don't give a fuck about you. They forget you. They forget us all within, say, two years or so. What do you do? You need to live. You have to pay the rent. Maybe this stage in our career is a conscious attempt to make a bit of money.

"In England, once you've been on 'Top of the Pops', once you've been on the cover of Smash Hits and you've had a top selling album in the charts, what's left? I mean, there's only so much you can do. You've been on national telly, that's more or less everyone's little ambition isn't it? What do you do after you've been on the cover of magazines? Conquer America? We were either going to split up or find something else to do. Touring the States and Canada seemed to be the only logical solution."

— David Steele—

JAPAN

—David Sylvian—

— Mick Karn —

"Romance is back in fashion but it's not meant to be taken seriously. It creates a mood. People have this desirable need to have a romantic relationship with someone. Everything starts getting out of hand when someone has a preconceived idea of how a relationship should work. Everyone wants to fall in love. It's quite in vogue, isn't it?"

— David Sylvian —

"I feel a lot of the bands coming out of England now aren't playing rock'n'roll, not for the last year or two anyways. I think it died a long long time ago although I don't think the term 'rock'n'roll' will ever go away. It'll be there forever, just like classical music. Someone should invent a new word or something. Rock'n'roll doesn't sound right anymore. It sounds like a cliché used for the wrong medium."

— Mick Karn —

SPARKS

— From left to right: Ronald Mael, Russell Mael —

"Our offstage personalities are very similar to what we're like in concert. I'm more outgoing, bouncier, and talkative. Ron's much more pensive, moodier, and intellectual about things. We really are the way we are in concert but it's probably more subtle in real life. By now we know each other's idiosyncracies. After a while you know what to say, and what not to say. We're beginning to feel optimistic because things are starting to open up in the States a bit, but as far as radio is concerned, we're still considered to be something of a threat. We don't know what's bothering them. If we knew, we would have solved the riddle twelve albums ago."

— Russell Mael —

NICO

"I studied with Lee Strasburg. He was very positive about my acting career because I could dissolve in front of the audience. I could dissolve into tears. It wasn't just related to performing an exercise in front of forty students within the class. It had a lot to do with my emotional state of mind. He felt I was one of the only ones and that gave me an awful lot of courage. Marilyn Monroe was in my class a year before she died. At that point in her career she was already worn out. But, in front, when she did her exercise, the scene, she was unbelievably fragile and afraid. She was like a windblown tree, just shaking all over her body. I couldn't believe it, such a big star to be so nervous. She even peed her dress. It could not be overlooked, since she never wore underpants. She peed her dress, yes, I'm not making it up."

LORDS of the NEW CHURCH

— Stiv Bator —

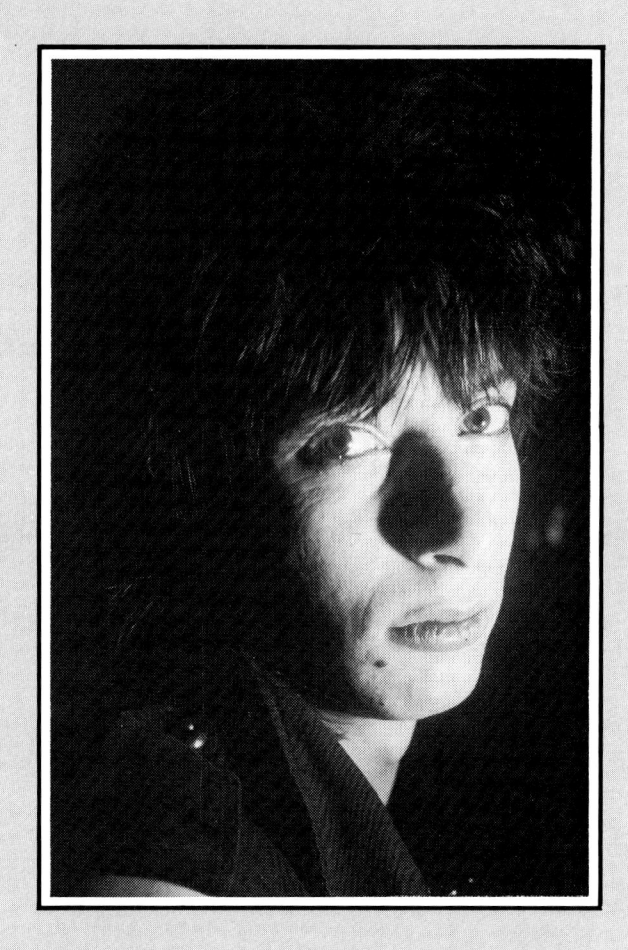

— Dave Tregunna —

— Nicky Turner —
— Brian James —

"Religions aren't destructive. It's the organizations, it's the Church. See, the Church originally started out as a gathering place for people, to learn the truths and to celebrate the things they believed in. Christ said, 'Never place one stone upon another in my honour.' Churches have grown into mind-controlled profiteering organizations. They're as bad as governments. It's all about power and control. What the New Church is about is that in the sixties when the youth had political power, right away drugs were infiltrated into it like L.S.D. and heroin. It screwed up everybody and eventually it was distorted through the media that that was what the music was about. So everyone followed all this hype instead of seeing what it was really about. They took the subversiveness out of it and controlled everyone. Then they brought in disco which turned everyone into mindless robots. When punk came out, its original intention was to break it down and get it back to the subversive element and let everybody do what they wanted. Again, the media distorted it by saying all punks were Nazis and that punks fight Teddy Boys on King's Road. They divide, conquered and split into different factions. Right now you have so many cults — skinheads, punks, Teddy Boys, heavy metal and electro boppers, and they're all supposed to hate each other because of the clothes they wear and the bands they listen to. The original idea was to unite people through music because you're young. It's a celebration of youth. And that's what the New Church is all about. We're here, this is a religious experience, probably the closest one in Western culture that you can feel spiritual satisfaction from. That's what voodoo's like, y'know, it's the drums, the rhythm and the shaman dancing. Everyone gets off on it together. That's the idea behind the New Church — bringing everyone together."

— Stiv Bator —

KaS PRODUCT

— Spatsz —   — Mona Soyoc —

"For us the record is totally different from the live show. It's got to be treated like a performance otherwise it won't work. I used to sing behind a plastic transparent sheet with lights casting my shadow from behind. Eventually I'd cut the sheet apart with razor blades. Suddenly, without warning, I'd pierce through the sheet towards the end of the song. When we play the song Underground Movie, I use a gun or a spear. Sometimes I just take a chair, sit down and face the audience. Once in a while we'll take two black sheets, about five meters long, and tie them to some support poles. We keep everything simple. When you're performing in a live situation I do think it's important to have something around you that creates an atmosphere. We like to work the stage totally different from the records. It's much more violent. In fact, sometimes I think I prefer our performances to our albums."

— Mona Soyoc —

THOMAS DOLBY

"At the moment we preconceive that music ought to consist of an arrangement with vocals over top of it and that a computer or a synthesizer should be played with a keyboard. I think that will change before very long because when you use a micro-computer to create music you're only using an enth of its total capacity. There are many different things you can do with a computer that are still musical. In the area of psycho-acoustics it's possible to trace the relationship between acoustic sounds and the actual emotions and moods that are triggered in a human being. The emotive quality of music, coming from acoustic instruments, has been dictated largely by the physical problems of getting sound waves through the air.

"I know that already in Japan there are people working with biorhythm machines where you can actually hook up your pulse rate, heart rate, eye movements or your respiration to a musical instrument and therefore use your body to create the music, which, in turn, would produce interesting reactions in anybody listening to it. One thing I'm really looking forward to is the day when I'll be able to plug an electrode into my brain and just think the music and let it come out that way."

SPOOONS

— Sandy Horne —

— Gordon Deppe —

—Derrick Ross—
— Rob Preuss —

"I imagine a house. Upon entering the front hall, I notice a very subtle chord in the air. It has always been there. I walk further into the house along the hallway and the chord begins to divide. With a little inspection, I discover that each note of the chord comes from a different room. Every room in the house has its own characteristic pitch. I pass through one of the doors and listen. Inside, the chord is nonexistent. I enjoy the solitary note for a while.

"Eventually I pull myself away and go back out through the hallway. The pieces of the chord rejoin. It is the last thing I hear as I leave."

— Gordon Deppe —

The CURE

— Lol Tolhurst — — Robert Smith —

— Simon Gallup —

"The Cure have never been in fashion so therefore we don't find the need to commit ourselves to a certain path and capitalize on that. In the time that we've known each other, we grew up and did a lot of different things. In that way, what we do as a group is not for the sake of a career, but as a group that reflects our way of life. That's the way it will always be. If it wasn't like that we wouldn't do it."

— Lol Tolhurst

BIG COUNTRY

— From left to right: Stuart Adamson, Mark Brzezicki, Tony Butler, Bruce Wilson —

"A group should be more like a gang rather than a group of people who got together on a commercial venture. The spirit of the group is much more important than the actual success of it. That's the way I've always felt about groups in general. The spirit and passion behind the music is more important than how well it does on the charts. If there's no spirit, then you're lying to yourself. There's no point having a group if you don't want it to be successful, but the feeling behind it is very important. Big Country gives me spirit, passion, adventure, but more importantly I discovered something about myself. I found a way of communicating with the members which is totally unique. I originally felt this in my previous group, the Skids, but then the spirit gradually faded away from it. Everyone seemed to drift apart. Suddenly the love for the original ideas disappeared into thin air. For something to sound proper, I think it's got to be done with love, feeling, and a passion. It should be the most important thing you could ever hope to do.

"Big Country is just a measure of the expanse of our ambitions. It's like a fictional place for us to discover and explore. A place for us to keep everything spread out over wide-open horizons. Our music does have a certain flavor. I mean, it does sound like Big Country. The name and the sound go hand in hand."

— Stuart Adamson —

X

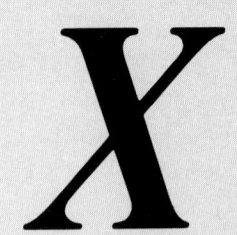

— From left to right: John Doe, Don Bonebrake, Exene Cervenka, Billy Zoom —

"There is a duality to Los Angeles. It's such a mixed up town. I mean, you never see any buttons that read 'I Love L.A.' because people who don't live there haven't a clue what it's like. We may point out the bad aspects of L.A. but we always have a lot of compassion for the people and the scene. It's not like the Fall or Public Image where everything's turned to shit. We've still got a lot of affection for the underground."

— John Doe —

JOHN FOXX

"At one time I thought making modern electronic disco music was the next logical development. I was tempted by it because I guess I was one of the first people to start doing it. I'm not interested in that anymore. Now I want to make my music very atmospheric. I like dance music because I occasionally like to go out and dance, but there's a lot more to explore than how to make people shuffle their feet, not that I despise that kind of music because there's a certain craftsmanship and artistry in that that's an absolutely wonderful one. But I also appreciate the other side of music as well. Right now I'm re-assessing some of the things Pink Floyd and people like that touched on in the late '60s. The fashion now is, of course, that all that is invalid, which is ridiculous because I don't think any kind of music is ever invalid. It all depends on how you choose the elements, how you arrange them and what you feel towards them.

"At the start of all these movements like the mods, hippies, and punks, there's a feeling of genuine excitement but it always tends to get lost and diluted much earlier than most people realize. As soon as the music's named, it's dead. And just before that, just when it's being born, it's wildly exciting. People usually make the mistake by trying to identify their identity too quickly. Listen, I would like to be popular, but I'm not going to change the way I do things in order to be popular."

The FIXX

— From left to right: Rupert Greenall, Adam Woods, Alfie Agius, Cy Curnin, Jamie West-Oram —

"When I wrote the lyrics for the Shuttered Room LP I was stuck in my front room with no money, watching television and slowly getting pissed off with the way documentaries are throwing supposed facts around to educate as well as entertain. Suddenly you become aware of the fact that so many things happen around you, incidents people tell you about after they've taken place or just before they're ready to happen. People just sit back and believe it. They even talk about it to their friends. Slowly you begin to realize everything is out of your control. I know it made me impotent. I wanted to find a way of making that impotence positive.

"This may sound strange but if I use a negative analogy about a certain situation, whenever that situation occurs, and I think about the negative side of it, I feel positive. The lyrics come about that way. I felt as if I was chained to the telly. It was as if the windowblinds were cutting me off from the outside world. Everyone's in their own little prison. You rush home from work, run into your house, lock the door and somehow you feel relaxed.

"You watch these programs and at first they appear to be quite normal and then all of a sudden you begin to get these really perverted ideas. They can blast into your head when you least expect it. You can't expect people to believe what they see on television, but the frightening thing is that they do. In believing it, all they're doing is replacing their individualism with someone else's ideas of what they should or shouldn't do. People have the power of making decisions but it's so easy to have somebody make them for you. It's the power of advertising. People want to be with the go-getters. It's martini advert time again."

— Cy Curnin —

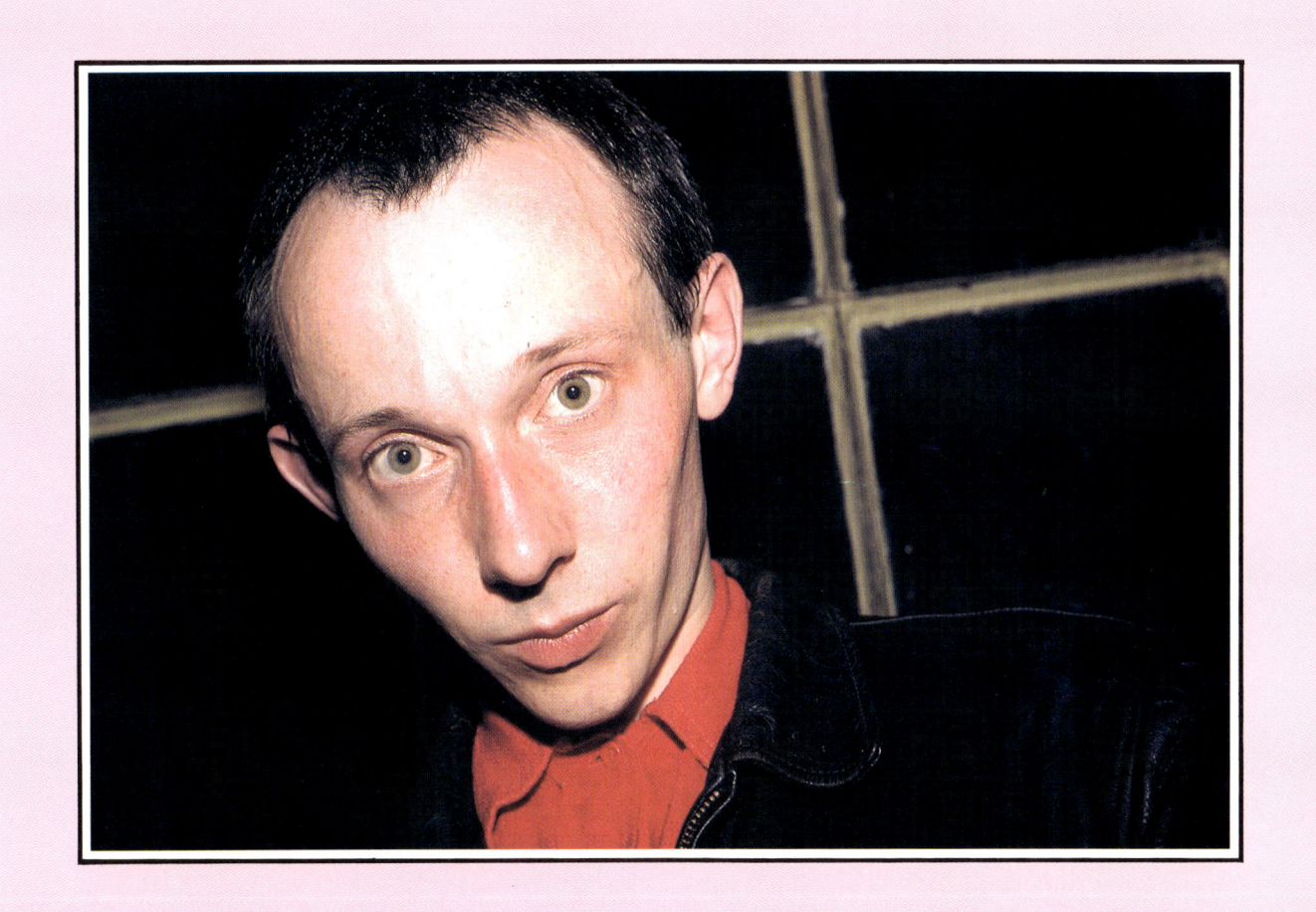

HOWARD DEVOTO

"I simply refuse to spell everything out, y'know, like this is Jack, this is Jill, and this is a synthesizer. Jack and Jill and the synthesizer. It sounds like a Swedish children's bedtime story, doesn't it?"

The BLASTERS

— Phil Alvin —   — John Bazz — — Gene Taylor —

76

— Dave Alvin — — Lee Allen — — Steve Berlin —

"We're typically an American band, not that an average band in America sounds like us. The sounds that have evolved over here, the ones that have grown throughout the twentieth century, represent the evolution of music. The British got in on the game 'coz they spoke the same language. The Germans did a lot of electronic music à la Stockhausen, and more recently with the likes of Tangerine Dream and Kraftwerk. The major influence came from America in the form of jazz and blues. It was the black and white mixture of two cultures. It's startin' to make itself coherent. We're startin' to understand our culture while we're still young.

"They've been playing Johnny B. Goode in bars ever since it came out. They might not write about it in Rolling Stone anymore, but people still love it. It's in their blood. It's like Beethoven's in the blood of some German guy. When he hears it, it's BEETHOVEN. For me it's Chuck Berry and Jimmy Reed. You wanna have culture. You wanna feel proud. So this guy's from Long Island. Be proud you're from Long Island. Good for you. Nuthin' wrong with Long Island... or Downey, California for that matter. Hell no! I'm proud to come from Downey, and besides, I like myself."

— Phil Alvin —

The BELLE STARS

— Stella Barker — Lesley Schone — — Jennie McKeown —
— Clare Hirst — Judy Parsons —

— Sarah-Jane Owen , Miranda Joyce —

"We don't necessarily think people have treated us differently just because we're an all-girl group. It's a difficult question to answer because we've never been in a situation to know what it's like other than being in an all-girl group. I think there might have been a difference in the early days when we couldn't play so well. You always get roadies and P.A. people who are would-be musicians anyways, and they're always jealous of anyone that's up onstage, especially with a women's group who've gone so far without having any musical background. Initially we were considered to be a novelty. Suddenly here was a seven-piece all-girl group who were touring England. Everyone looked at us as if we were a band of penguins. It's not so much a novelty anymore because now there's lots of girl groups. Now we're treated quite professionally. The cynics have finally realized we can play."
— Sarah-Jane Owen —

"I suppose we want to achieve success by doing the kind of material that we, as a band, want to do without compromising our artistic integrity. I think that's any band's idea, really. There's always compromise within the Belle Stars. I mean, just by being in a band of seven people, we've had to make compromises. In a way it's good because there's no one person's music going out. Each person contributes their own ideas. We have a voting system. It's very democratic. It's a good job we're a seven-piece and not an eight-piece, otherwise…"
— Stella Barker —

JOEY RAMONE

"Yeah, I guess a lot of groups do copy us, but y'know, everyone's a copy of someone else anyways. I mean, Costello copies Springsteen and Springsteen copies Van Morrison. It just goes on and on. And that band called Horse... Y'know the group that sings about America? Horselips, yeah that's it! I even heard they're doing a version of Blitzkrieg Bop."

HOLLY BETH VINCENT

"Wait a minute, I'm not Joan Jett or anybody else! Why compare me with another female performer? Can't you find someone else's career that's suddenly taken off? Why does it always have to be another girl? What the hell is this thing about being a girl musician anyways? The problem I have with my career is the fact that I know what I want. I write my own music, therefore, I do have an immense amount of control over what I do. A lot of the men I deal with can't handle it. I've split with my manager. My record company even dropped me because they thought I was impossible to work with. Okay, maybe I happen to think in a way that's a bit unorthodox. Maybe I have done a few things that have been a bit off the wall. I'm more like an Iggy Pop rather than a Joan Jett. If you want to compare careers, he's a guy whose been around for ages. Maybe I'll be around for ages too and never really be enormous.

"I think I'm a reasonably intelligent person. I like calling the shots. I'd like to find a manager who's more intelligent than myself, someone who knows the business better than I do and then I might listen to him. I just can't listen to people who don't know what they're talking about. Nobody's been able to classify Holly Beth Vincent. They're finding it difficult to accept that I'm me and that I'm not fronting a punk or heavy metal band. Every album I make will probably be drastically different from the next one. Maybe that's what prevented me from getting deals. I remember the time when I went up to the A&R people in my former record company and said, 'Listen, if you're expecting me to write the same thing year after year, you can forget it!'"

— Holly Beth Vincent —

BAD BRAINS

— Darryl Jenifer —
— Earl Hudson —

— H.R. —
— Dr. Know —

"You see all these senators and politicians who have the audacity to say that they're Christians. They go in there, man, and they try to use God and all these other good qualities that they don't possess and then they take money from us and use it against us. They even use the Bible against us. Now, in these last days of time, men of power thrive on corruption. They think it's cool to be evil and icked. That's what they do in America, although they try to pretend In God We Trust. Everybody knows there's not one politician you could ever trust, especially in America.

"I've lived in Washington all my life. If you ever seen the cynical, disgusting, sad way they try to pretend they're American citizens you'd puke your guts out on national television. Ain't no such thing as an American anyways. The real Americans are the Indians and they don't ever want to be called that word."

— H.R. —

JAMES BLOOD ULMER

"Like I just told you — I made a record called Black Rock and CBS put the damn thing on the jazz shelf so I don't really know the answer to your question. I know I play the same way. I figure I'm a jazz guitarist but my band ain't jazz, that's for sure. They're much too young to know about jazz. I make sure of that. Y'know what I mean, it's from the heart. They only know jazz by hearing it, not by livin' it. You have to be born into that era to really understand it. If you were born before 1940 you would know about jazz whether you played an instrument or not. The guys that play with me know more about rhythm and blues. I mix my style of jazz with their spontaneity. I try to create a modulation between jazz, rock, funk, and all the other musics at the same time.

"The difference between the way I play guitar and the way most rock guitarists play is that I don't play rock'n'roll. These rock'n'roll guys — I mean, they don't necessarily even know how to play. I play more of a jazz guitar. Now if you're talkin' about the music, now see, that's different! The music and the way I play guitar are totally different from one another. I'm playing a harmolotic type of music. I'm playing a music where each individual is stating more than one thing at the same time. That's what harmolotic means — MORE, MORE, MORE... Instead of having one wife, let's say you have four, then you're harmolotic!"

FASHION

— Dik Daviss —

— Mulligan —

— De Harriss —
— Martin Recchi —

Mulligan: "We're not particularly trying to say anything political. That's the difference between what we were like in 1979 and the way we are now. When we appeared in Toronto in '79, we thought we had messages and we were putting across points with songs like Hanoi Annoys Me and Technofascist. We were going through a phase where we tried to make a lot of statements. The statement we wanna make now is, 'Enjoy this for god's sake. It's dance music!' I'm not telling everybody we're going to give them a real fun time. We're saying this is meant to be a show and people can attend it so they can get some enjoyment out of it. We're making dance music. We don't want you to look at yourselves. It's the same as when you were at a Hendrix concert. I mean, you didn't stand there asking yourself, 'Uh, do I have my head on right?' It's the power and the feeling that you get. Look at the way Hendrix's charisma affected everyone. Anything he'd play would completely tantalize the audience. You would be so intrigued by what he was going to do next, y'know, in the way he was playing, the style, the feeling and the power. This is what groups of today should be about. A pop group should thrive on raw energy."

Daviss: "Yeah, Mulligan's right. Rock changed nothing, politically speaking. It just gave people an excuse to wear different clothes and have a good time. That's the whole thing about it, isn't it? Dress up, have a dance, pick up a few women and take some drugs?"

Mulligan: "The only thing that's changed is before it used to be sex and drugs and rock'n' roll, and now it's sex and coke and funk."

LENE LOVICH

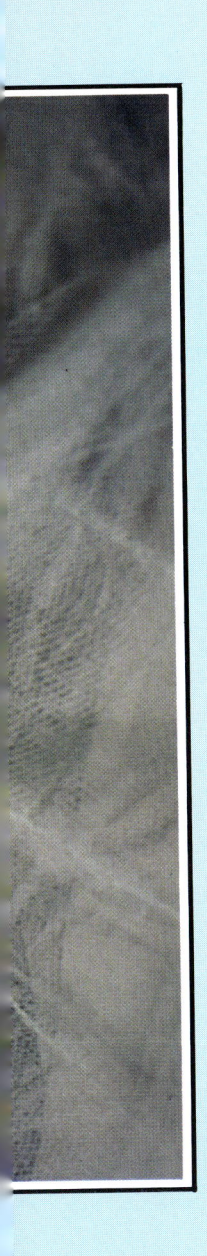

— From left to right: Lene Lovich, Les Chappell —

Lene: "I don't really think of myself as a man or a woman."

Les: "I do."

Lene: "Especially when I'm not performing onstage. It never enters my head, what sex I am. Never. When I perform I get a feeling of great strength. I feel a massive exchange between the audience and myself. . . . But it's much more than that. I get the best results when I throw a little bit of energy out to the audience because they usually throw a lot more back to me. It's the exchange of energy that's exciting. You see, I'm so happy when I'm onstage because I feel as if it's my world, and in my world I can really be myself. It's much more difficult in the outside world. I suppose I feel like I've been a minority all my life. When I'm performing I sense this feeling of complete freedom. I feel strong."

APB

— From left to right: Nick Jones, Iain Slater, Glenn Roberts, George Cheyne —

"There's loads of new groups popping up all over Scotland. Heaps! A lot of it has to do with the music papers. They blow everything out of proportion. One week they said, 'This month Scottish bands are in.' Next thing you know everybody starts taking notice of them. They used to write all these fab articles on the Postcard groups like the Fire Engines and Orange Juice. It was just a lot of hype. Some silly reporter got it in his head and then the next week the big thing was Birmingham bands. APB never went for that Scottish novelty stuff. We kept a low profile in those days.

"About three years ago Glenn Roberts [APB's guitarist] and I went to France for a holiday. We checked out some of the discos over there. Up until then we'd been listening to mostly punk stuff like the Pistols and The Clash. The French discos exposed us to a lot of heavy American funk. We immediately got hooked on the sound. It was great to dance to. We just walked in and had a wonderful time. Since then we buy funk records whenever we get the chance. George Clinton from Bootsy Collins is my hero. I like black funk stuff. I love the way it feels. There's nothing like it in the world."

— Iain Slater —

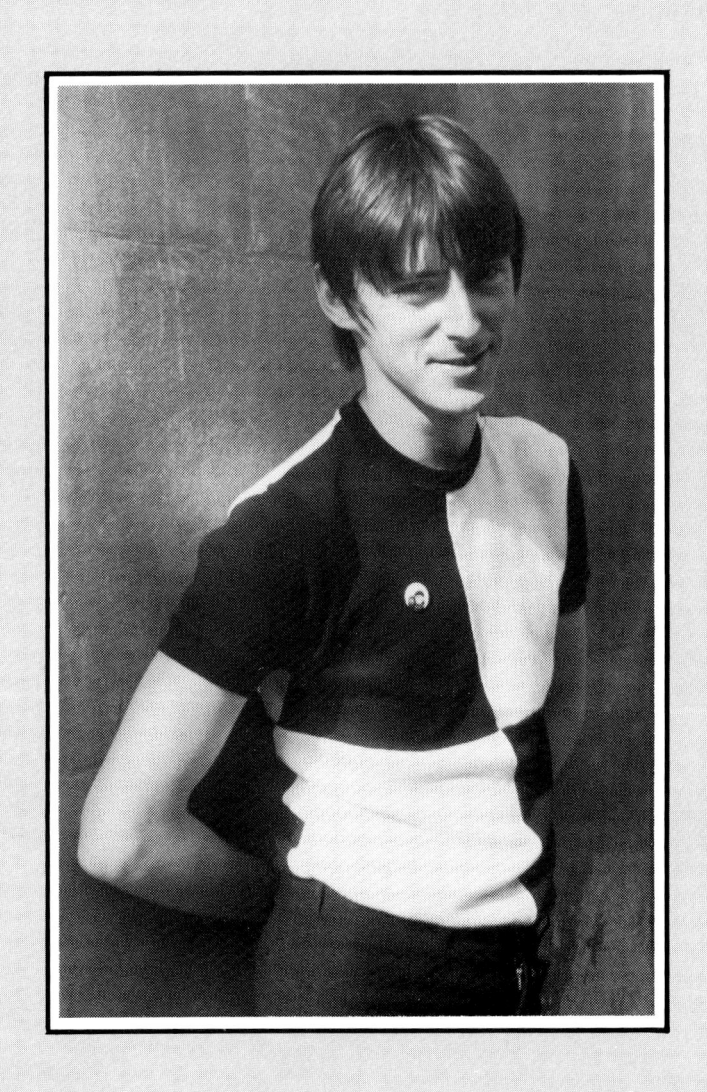

The STYLE COUNCIL

"A lot of people said the reason why The Jam never broke the States was because they were too British for American audiences. Well, I think that was bullshit. It sounded like some glib excuse to me. Critics felt uncomfortable with the kind of music we were representing at the time because it was different. It never was a part of the mainstream rock tradition that America follows. People felt alienated from it. It challenged them and most people didn't want to be challenged. People prefer familiarity, so why not go into a record shop and buy an album which you know you're going to like anyways? It's much easier. That's why heavy metal music is so popular. There's nothing in that kind of music that will challenge their values, ideals, and conceptions of what music should be like."

— Paul Weller —

PETE SHELLEY

"I can't imagine why some people wouldn't like electronic music. Some people think it's the devil's music. In Sweden I heard that the socialist party said synthesizer music is very right wing. It's happening all over. People have these really odd ideas. It's more like witchcraft to some people. The electronic medium frightens them. It's just like when the Beatles came over and people used to say, 'Oh no! They play electric guitars. There's no feeling in electric guitars!' The same thing is happening with electronic music. People are saying it doesn't have any feeling and it won't catch on. Even if it becomes more widespread it'll be a good thing because in a few years it'll be far cheaper to build a synthesizer than it will a guitar. Everyone will be able to have an electronic musical instrument within their reach. It's just like the punk explosion in '77. People who never played an instrument before will suddenly be able to pick up a Casio VL Tone and they'll write and play their own songs."

PYLON

— Michael Lachowski —   — Randy Bewley —   — Curtis Crowe —
— Vanessa Ellison —

"Being a young group from Georgia, we came at it from a whole different standpoint than most bands. We were going to play New York once, break up and go back to school, paint or whatever. There are a lot of people in bands who take the opposite viewpoint of, 'I'm gonna be a star by next month. I will settle for nothing less than complete stardom and absolute control over my audience.' They just go around in circles wondering why they didn't make it as a big star. It could be because they were either assholes or just flatout bad musicians. Regardless, if they fall flat on their ass they hurt a lot worse. So we just said we'll go as far as we can possibly go and then when it falls apart..."

— Curtis Crowe —

BREEDING GROUND

— Jonathan Strayer —   — Hugh Gladish —   — John Shirreff —   — Ken Jones —

"Louis was a Hemidrone, or at least, the soul of the Hemidrones. What inspired him to move on, was his secret. In the wake of his relocation, three old friends inseparable and another of the limbs rejected. Breeding Ground. Picking up where Louis left off, until perhaps, we realize why he left in the first place. I should sit down with him one day and discuss his secret."

— John Shirreff —

STING

"Rock'n'roll in America is as dead as a dodo. I blame it on the radio stations whom I find too secretarian in their playlists. You could turn on any radio station, hear a certain type of music, and five minutes later you'd be hearing the same music in a different song by another artist. It's so homogeneous that it's unlistenable. Everything sounds the same because there's no crossover between musical forms. There's no interface, no spark. All you get are rigid lines and the music rarely steps over the existing boundaries. That's why bands like Foreigner, Styx, and Boston all sound like ten-year-old groups. They all sound like Yes. Obviously they're very good at what they're doing but they're not making any leaps or bounds or even thinking about sounding new. And it's because of American radio. People are being brainwashed. It's all controlled by industry. They want to sell washing powder, jeans, and cars and they programme their records to make certain people buy them. I mean, it's almost as if a computer has decided what kind of music toothpaste buyers will listen to."

PULSALLAMA

— From left to right back row: Jean Caffeine, Miss April Palmieri, Judy Sleaze, Wendy Wild. Front row: Min "Bonefinder" Thometz, Kimberly "Princess" Davis, Stace "Timbalina" Elkin —

"Pulsallama started out as a joke that was never intended to last. We were a group of girls who'd do parties around New York at different clubs. That's how we got to know each other. Once there was a benefit for a club [Club 57] that we all originally met at around '79/'80. We decided to do a band number for the benefit. Everyone really liked it so we decided to do it again. Eventually we bought instruments and learned how to play them 'coz we were originally banging away on beer bottles, pots and pans.

"We have a crazy sense of humor. Have you heard us? We're not a serious band that gets up there and sings real heavy lyrics. We're not concerned about how perfect our live sound is. We just want to have a lot of fun when we're on stage. We're percussive but we don't play like other percussive bands. We don't even have a guitar. On one of our songs the bassist, the singer and the drummer all do the exact same thing. That's a taboo in music. People aren't supposed to do that sort of thing. We do weird things like that because we're not musicians. We really don't know the right ways of making music and maybe that's why we sound the way we do.

"What's kept us together and interested in what we're doing is that we're all good friends. We've kept everything light and fun. It's a lot of work. We've got problems and complications just like every other band does. If we stop getting along, if the fun stops, that's when it will end."

— Min "Bonefinder" Thometz —

RICHARD HELL

"I actually recorded a Frank Sinatra song. I'll play it for you when we go back to my apartment. I was originally going to put it on the first album but it was a little shaky. Yeah, I'm an admirer of Frank Sinatra. I decided to do a rendition of All The Way. It's a song I've loved for years and years. He sings it so well. I recorded it on the original demos for the Blank Generation album but when the time came to pick the final songs, I decided to drop it. I love to listen to Frank's good songs. I'm no afficianado fan or anything. I mean, it's not like I don't know anything in particular about his life-style. He's good. Anybody who hits a photographer is okay by me."

— Richard Hell —

JOAN JETT

"When I look back on it now I can't believe people had the attitude that girls couldn't rock'n'roll. It just strikes me as being a ridiculous thought. But yeah, the Runaways were rock'n'roll martyrs because in those days we used to take so much shit from the business. And we took shit from a lot of the other bands that we had to play with. If I remember correctly we used to have a lot of trouble with Rush."

LOUNGE LIZARDS

"I was responsible for calling our music 'Fake Jazz' and somehow I wish I had never come up with such a silly term; all the critics are taking it so seriously. I knew the traditional jazz critics were going to come down on us. None of the Lizards are trying to compare with the best sax player or bassist in the jazz field. We have nothing to do with that scene. In terms of jazz I don't give a damn who has the best chops. I mean, chops is not an appealing feature; I don't care for musicians with chops. Chops is a jazz term which represents technical proficiency. I want to be technically proficient but chops indicates that you have to be technically apt in a specific mode. I decided to call our music fake jazz because it's supposed to be meaningless. If you analyze it for thirty seconds it loses its validity. When all of these articles came out describing what fake jazz was, I was no longer interested in it as a term. Surprisingly enough, only about 25 percent of our audience is hardcore jazz fans.

"Why am I suddenly having to deal with record company people? I mean, I'm poor anyway. I'd rather be poor than be associated with the slimiest people on earth."

— John Lurie —

BERNARD SZAJNER

"How do you play live when you cannot play an instrument? The logical solution was to try and invent my own instruments instead of learning how to play a traditional instrument. That's how I started on the Laser Harp and the Snark. It was a natural progression for me because I'm an audio-visual technician and I used to create music from light sources [slide projectors, lasers etc.]

"The Laser Harp is not at all like the Snark. It's called a harp because it's a triangular-shaped instrument. It has a flat surface of light and photo-electric cells inside. If you put your hand on this flat surface it will create a shadow, the photo-electric cells will analyze it, and it'll trigger certain sounds. After a while I found it was very difficult to put my hand in a precise position on the surface. That's why I came up with the idea of constructing laser beams as if they were strings. Now the actual instrument has a total of ten beams. Seven of them are used to control the notes. Each beam has a photo-electric cell at the end of it which analyzes light or no light. It's very binary. It's like a switch on a keyboard. The other three beams control the envelopes which affect the varied filters. Because the beams are V-shaped, the lower you go the closer the beams will be. With the same surface of hand you can intercept all the beams simultaneously. This will change the entire scale. The lower you go, the higher you will go on the music scale. The Laser Harp is a two-dimensional instrument. A regular keyboard is usually played one-dimensionally because you can play it from left to right [horizontally]. The great thing about the harp is not only can you play it horizontally, but you can also play it up and down [vertically]. The fact that you can play two-dimensionally means that you'll be able to cover a scale of twelve octaves instantly with both hands. It's just like having a gigantic keyboard.

"As I'm playing the Laser Harp everything will become more complicated to a point where the sound will become totally abstract. It's just like taking a block of sound as if it were a piece of clay and twisting it, bending it, tearing it apart and putting it back together. After a while I'll move my hands very slightly and they'll begin to make huge variations throughout the sounds. I've seen audiences become fascinated when they see how one subtle movement can create gigantic variations in one sound. This expands their way of perceiving sound. Most rock music is basically made up of beat after beat with very strong simple effects thrown in. I've noticed that even rock audiences can take a few minutes of totally abstract music, music that doesn't have any rhythm or melodic structure that they can identify with. They'll be able to take this abstract mass of sound and find their own way into it."

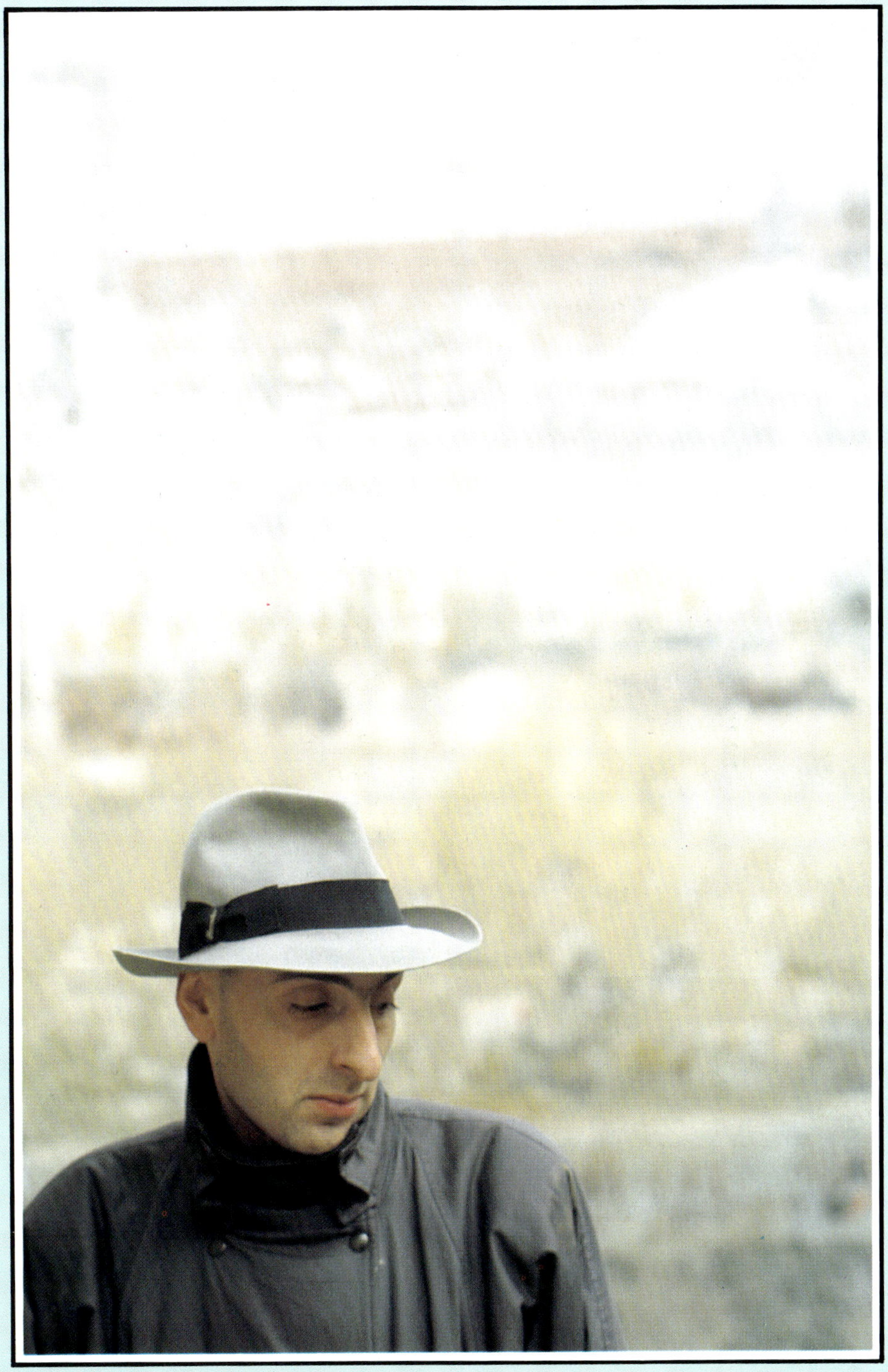

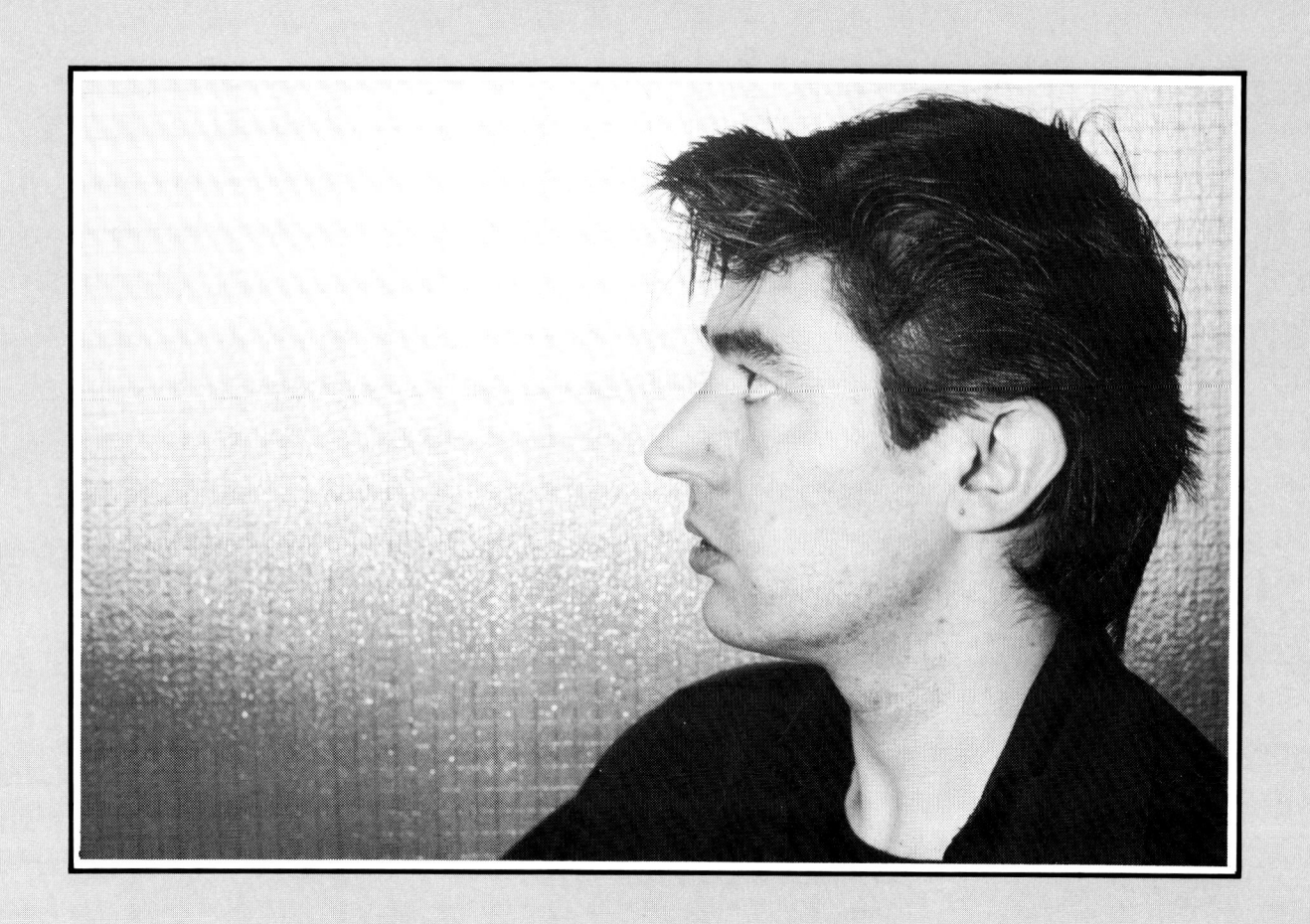

CHRIS SPEDDING

"The rock field is getting about as conservative as country music now, in trying to conserve a sort of fantasy in the way it ought to be, which is not the spirit of rock'n'roll at all. Today's trash is tomorrow's art, which is what all the Presley things were. I'm talking about the very early ones, Sun Records and so on. That feeling, today's trash is tomorrow's art, is very much the disco thing. Everyone who thinks they've got good taste believes that disco is sheer trash. You just wait: in a few years' time, when all the best stuff comes out, everyone will suddenly realize how wonderful the best of the disco stuff really was. People will write treatises on it just like they did with Presley. When he sustained himself for twenty years, everybody decided he was alright."

The BIRTHDAY PARTY

"The sheer physical fact of playing in front of an audience can be quite a dehumanizing process, where, bit by bit, what may have once been an 'honest performer' gradually develops an onstage image that ends up being totally different from his or her own personality. There just seems to be so much pressure put on various performers to succumb to the fantasies of the rock press, their audiences and so on, that eventually, even in their day-to-day lives, it's not just becoming one personality at home, which is bad enough, but it just becomes this one onstage personality all the time until it becomes very unhealthy. It's essential to keep a firm grasp on your own personality and individuality. If someone is put in the situation where there is a great deal of attention focused upon them by means of the press and the imaginations of the audience, his character will be overexaggerated to such a great extent that he'll feel as if he has to live up to this expectation, and eventually, he'll turn into a living parody of himself.

"I find it very difficult to remain honest with myself when all I know the audience wants me to be is entertaining and exciting. The moment I begin to pander to an audience and give them what they want, I lose respect for myself. For me, a good performance is to remain honest from beginning to end. A great performance for me could be one where I'm totally still. Everyone always expects the Birthday Party to provide them with a very physical, violent show. I can't say that I find performing in front of an audience to be a joyful experience. Quite often I don't feel as if I'm in the mood to perform. And so it is unfortunate when the audience comes to see the Birthday Party when certain members don't feel like performing. Because we're an unprofessional outfit, and we have no particular way of behaving onstage, very often our audiences will be subjected to very boring, tedious concerts. We will not put on an act for anyone."

— Nick Cave —

DURAN DURAN

— From left to right: Roger Taylor, Andy Taylor, John Taylor (top), Simon Le Bon, Nick Rhodes —

"Everybody wants to look good. Kids from the age of twelve and up save their pocket money so they can buy some new clothes. It makes them feel marvelous really. That's how this band got together in a sense. When everyone was wandering around in torn-up jeans, ripped T-shirts and dirty sneakers, we wanted to look good. There's a reason behind dressing up. It's fun. I think people put far too much importance on it. They try to make it seem more significant than it really is."

— Simon Le Bon —

TAXI GIRL

— Daniel Darc —   — Mir Wais —

"I don't want to sound as if I'm putting down my own country, but I really don't think rock'n roll has anything to do with France. Bands like us only sell records to a specific audience. Nobody else seems to be interested. We could easily blame it on European radio but what good would that do? They're just playing the same old tunes. That's why so many alternative new music French bands eventually have to break up. Maybe Taxi Girl are a rare exception, I don't know. We can do something in France but we need time. You've got to understand that France really doesn't have a pop culture it can call its own. We've got the '50s and the '60s to look back on, but, even then, that didn't have anything to do with the French way of life. It was all American influences like Elvis Presley and Gene Vincent.

"It's funny, we receive a lot of fan mail full of spelling mistakes, bad grammar and so on. The words in most rock music are so dumb and the people who idolize this music must be pretty dumb too. When you listen to a heavy rock French group like Trust, it's just political nonsense and it's not even well written. We're going to try and change that in French music. We want to sing about things that people can benefit from. I mean, we won't prostitute our art, but we do want to be listened to. And maybe if we're listened to we'll be able to offer them something that's got some sense of meaning, of being. Maybe the Human League are more important than the Monochrome Set — not because they're better, that's false. A lot of people listen to them. Maybe their music can change people just by one word or a certain phrasing, but if you really listen closely, it doesn't change anyone or anything. Change is important. We could easily play the kind of music that would make people happy and drink a lot of beer to, but that isn't our intention. We have a role I think. A responsibility."

— Daniel Darc —

MINNY POPS

— Second and third from left: Wally Van Middendorp and Wim Dekker (only original members left) —

"It's the same old story for independent groups. It's the organizational problem within the structure of the music business which hasn't been changed for a good ten years. There's no possibility of meeting open-minded people in the major companies who have new ideas. People have to take chances by starting their own magazine or record label, and we all know how difficult that can be. There have been people out there who've been playing D.J. for ten years and the sad thing is they never move up. They just compromise within their programming and play a small portion of new alternative music. I call it playing it safe. That's exactly what's happening in Holland. There are no A&R people in the record companies who are willing to take the time to check out new groups. It's universal. Change is the only solution. I think everyone's going to be in for a big surprise."

— Wally Van Middendorp —

JOHN CALE

"I've got a lot of respect for Captain Beefheart. Apart from being a musician, he's one of the best illustrators in the world. You see this guy, he comes in here, you give him a sheet of paper and you ask him to draw something. What the guy does with a pen is ridiculous. I saw the Christmas cards he used to send to the guys at Warner Brothers — works of art, beautiful illustrations. Drop of the hat. I've never seen Beefheart actually perform, although I opened for him on a tour in France. I met him in the foyer of the hotel and I said, 'Hey Don, are you still painting, man?'

"He said, 'Are you kidding? After what they did to me in music?'

"He'd given up."

DEAD KENNEDYS

— From left to right: Klaus Flouride, East Bay Ray, Jello Biafra, D. H. Peligro —

"We've got to make the American people aware of what's going on in El Salvador so it doesn't turn into another Viet Nam. And if it doesn't turn into another Viet Nam, at least it'll make people realize there are certain individuals in this country who'd like to find another Viet Nam by testing various places to see what will work. Carter tried Afghanistan. Eventually Reagan tried El Salvador. I guess maybe the coffee industry didn't pay him enough bribes... so now he's looking at Libya."

— Jello Biafra —

KING SUNNY ADE

"We've recorded over forty albums but only one has been released in North America (Ju Ju Music). It's nobody's fault really. Everything has its own time and place. We didn't have any connections before. People weren't so sure they were interested in records from Africa, let alone Nigeria. But now that we've signed with Island, we're going to try to get to the people. Nobody wanted to listen to us back then. They thought they were taking a risk. Ju Ju music is real traditional — the only difference is that we put modern technology into it. I think finally the people are showing that they're interested.

"I first wanted to play music when I was fourteen years old. I always loved music. I would go from school and listen to one of the local bands. All I wanted to do was participate. Whenever they went on a break I just loved to touch their drums. Today, I love music to the extent that I have to play music before I go to sleep. Let's say I wanted to hear some music before I go to sleep tonight — I'll turn on the telly. If it doesn't play any music then I'll turn on a radio. If there isn't any radio I'll have to go somewhere else to hear something. I have about two or three tape recorders when I'm on the road. I love playing music but my family didn't really like the idea at the beginning. Now, all over Nigeria and the rest of Africa, parents are finally allowing their children to play music that they're interested in. In the olden days they never showed their appreciation or encouragement. I ran away from school to join a group. My parents wanted me to be a lawyer or an engineer, someone people could point to and say, 'He's doing fine.' I just decided that I had to play music. I had no idea it was going to be like this."

PUBLIC IMAGE LTD.

— Keith Levene —

— John Lydon —

"PiL wants to be hardest fucking band in existence, musically speaking that is. I think, at the moment, we are — not just musically, but as a band. PiL is what bands are all about. Miles Davis is unbelievable, right? So are the Swollen Monkeys. Miles nearly did it but not quite. The Beatles were the hardest band of them all. The Stones nearly were because they rapped up on what the Beatles did. Since then it hasn't really happened. It almost happened with the Sex Pistols but it didn't. It's very difficult to put PiL's motives into words. I mean, I could put it into words but I'm not going to intellectualize about it 'coz it's just not that big a deal. Our music isn't specifically aimed for only rock'n'roll people, it's for all people.

"The original thing about PiL was that we weren't a band, we were a company. Now we're like three companies under one roof. We've expanded and grown much bigger. Public Image Ltd. was our first company. PEP [Public Enterprise Productions] was created because we needed our very own record/production company. Our third company, MIC [Multi Image Corporation], produces PiL's music and coordinates various artistic projects which involve computer graphics, electronics and video. I guess you could call it the first commercial co-op. It facilitates a lot more than what we achieved in the past.

"We always wanted to do more things than just play musical instruments. We couldn't do it with PiL. We were having a terrible time with the record companies and the thing we were saying all along was how a record company should do it, so we just said, 'We'll be a record company and do it ourselves.'"

— Keith Levene —

"In England, before you get involved in anything, you've got to conform to a standard listening procedure. People want to know, Now how can I relate to this? What style of clothes can I adopt with this music? Will it be good for my cool to like it?

"The only reason we're interested in being in a group is because, at first, it was an escape from the monotony of life. I just think people must be completely mad to want to see us in the first place. The aspirations of being taken seriously make the whole situation seem so absurd."

— John Lydon —

JULIAN COPE

"If you're going to be in a group it's only natural you're going to have a big ego, or else you wouldn't be able to stand on stage and sing your own songs. If someone were to say, 'Y'know, that Jerry Dammers guy of the Specials? Well, he's got a big ego,' I would accept that because of what he's done. Things get uncomfortable when people are maniacs with their egos. Maybe I do have a big ego but at least I'm aware of how funny and ironic it is being in a pop group. To me it's as if it's one big game. The thing is, I get excited about things where people think it's uncool to get excited. It really used to piss me off when we performed on 'Top of the Pops.' There were all these people trying to be beautiful. I mean, I was trying to do the same, trying to look good for the show. Everyone walked past each other trying so desperately to avoid the other person just in case they saw someone who looked better than they did, something that would spoil their ego. I just stare at everybody. Who can be bothered with being cool all of the time? Listen, I know what's going on. I'm not thick. I'm not just some deadhead pop singer."

JIM CARROLL

"I became close friends with John Belushi just a couple of years before he passed away. Y'know, it was funny, he really hated the image of being adored by fraternities. He was absolutely crazy. He was always looking for the outrageous, the extreme. He loved to test people's balls — see how gullible people really were. It's kind of ironic now, but he used to have a strong liking for a song that I wrote on the Catholic Boy album. It was called People Who Died. When he used to listen to it he would virtually freak out on the spot. I mean, he loved it. He used to make a point of dropping by at our rehearsals just so that he could play it on the drums.

"Now I've added a new verse to the song which is dedicated to John. I guess I'm probably going to think about him every time I play that song. Yeah, he was a friend of mine."

BLANCMANGE

—Stephen Luscombe—

—Neil Arthur—

Stephen: "You have to have some sort of intellectual reason for actually existing according to the New Musical Express. The fact that we haven't, the fact that we just do it and say that we do it and there's no political or intellectual reason, apart from the fact that we enjoy doing it and we enjoy people who are enjoying our music, well, that isn't good enough for the N.M.E., I'm afraid."

Neil: "And that's the best reason in the world to be doing anything! I just don't mean music, it can be anything your heart desires."

Stephen: "We're not the kind of people who attempt to put some sort of important message across to the world in our music 'coz we haven't got an important message. That's left to the politicians and people who are better qualified to do that than we are."

Neil: "But why does a musician have to justify what it is that he's doing? It's ridiculous. I mean, obviously there's always a legitimate reason for doing something..."

Stephen: "I know it's important in an interview to explain more or less how you are, obviously, otherwise there would be no point in doing an interview, but for people to sort of look for hidden reasons or reasons which are considered to be important in the eyes of certain periodicals..."

Neil: "I just can't understand it. People take music so seriously. It's like the most important thing in the world to them. It isn't. There are so many other things that matter."

Stephen: "I really don't know why I get such a kick out of making music. There's no way I can describe it. Neil and I work on the same set-up at both of our homes. We sort of swap sketches every now and then, put them together and see how they work. We've got our own little portable studio consoles. Sometimes we'll sit there for days and nothing will come out. Suddenly I'll get this incredible shiver down my spine and I'll think to myself, 'This is wonderful. I love it. I really want other people to hear it,' and I'll do it for no other reason than that."

RICK JAMES

— Rick James and acquaintance Beth Bovaird —

"If I was outside Rick James, I would buy Rick James's records. He's an interesting concept. Maybe it's because he's playing a kind of black music that hasn't been explored before. It's got a lot to do with the application of different sound transfers to the medium of R&B. The only other black group I ever heard that was really innovative on a sound transfer was Sly and the Family Stone. Rick James's sound transfers from a lot of idioms including rock'n'roll, blues, funk, and jazz. It's the application of transferring sounds you've grown up with into frequencies aligned to your own means of communication. Shit, it's got a lot to do with changes. Take the punk movement for example. When it got hooked up with fashion everything got exciting. It wasn't very different from what happened in the past but it was needed. It came about when disco was dying out. Hippies cut their hair and suddenly they were dressing like businessmen. They all went around looking like John Travolta. New Wave brought everybody back into lunacy. It made things interesting again."

DAVID THOMAS

— from left to right: Mayo Thompson, Tony Maimone, David Thomas, Alan Ravenstine, Scott Krauss —

"We couldn't even draw more than two hundred people in Cleveland. The kids there wanted hard, driving rock singers with crotch-tight pants and screaming fucking maniacs. So we had to get out of Ohio and go play on the road, even if it meant we were going to lose a lot of money. In Cleveland you either surrender to the game or you go play in the basement."
—David Thomas —

BILL NELSON

"To sit down and talk about my music and rationalize; for me it seems to defeat the object. Everything that I've done has happened naturally and organically. I've been accused by people, particularly in the British press, of being precocious and pretentious. Now, pretention seems to denote some kind of unnatural intent that's completely outside your own personal reference, trying to be something that you're not. Everything I've done seems to have happened of its own accord and then afterwards I've rationalized. You learn much more after the event by looking back and then calculating what happened. Why did I feel that way? How come that particular lyric had a fascination for me? I'm just beginning to look at life much differently now. I'm starting now, gradually, at this late date I suppose, to find out what place I have in the scheme of things, not in terms of commercial success but what my creative voice is and that it does have a point of view. An individual voice is important regardless of whether it achieves as much as someone else's. The fact that it's individual and is heard by some people is important."

RICHARD STRANGE

"As an idea, Cabaret Futura was about attempting to dignify an audience by accepting that their appreciation of an evening's entertainment could extend beyond the concentration span of two rock bands on stage and that's it. If you present something that is done with thought, care, and a positive spirit you can involve and embrace an audience. The reason why I initially opened the Futura Club in London was because I didn't want to play rock clubs anymore. I didn't want to undertake massive tours but I did want to play occasionally. The ideal solution would be to find a space that I could operate once a week which had fairly rudimentary facilities, like a bar, a stage, and a couple of anterooms where you could withdraw from all the noise and talk, which I find to be an extremely important part of an evening out.

"Instead of just calling it a rock club and involving dance, video, comedy, performance art, poetry, and music and pushing it to a rock crowd, we went the other route by trying to pull in an audience that wasn't exclusively rock oriented. The most important thing a rock show can do is not what's coming off the stage but what it generates within an audience. Rock'n'roll has long held itself to be a great revolutionary force, but I think it's probably the most conservative of all popular art forms. Possibly it's just something that occurs on a Saturday night where two people in the audience meet each other and off they go. The music is only an excuse. It's the catalyst."

KILLING JOKE

— From left to right: Dave Raven, Geordie, Jaz Coleman, Paul Ferguson —

"We enjoy making an awful sound. I think it's rather glorious. It sums up the temporary environment. It's not going to last. I see the forthcoming changes, whether they be a nuclear holocaust or natural disaster, as an excellent opportunity for change. People's senses are completely dulled. Their intelligence is directed into their food, not having dandruff and keeping their breaths fresh with mouthwash. I call it self-conscious paranoia. When all of this shit disappears, I see it as an excellent opportunity to break down all the conditions that have been destroyed. We'll be able to strip down individuals to their basic personalities. Then it'll be a matter of finding an environment where people can progress. Most people are usually discouraged from doing certain things because they think it's pure fantasy. Listen, there's no such thing as fantasy. It's a word of restriction used by people who look at it as a form of ridicule and are frightened to give up their security."

—Geordie—

IGGY POP

"I'd like to read to you an intro to Celine's Journey To The End of Night.

'Travel is a good thing. It stimulates the imagination. Everything else is a snare and a delusion. Our own journey is entirely imaginative. Therein lies its strength. It leads from life to death. Men, beasts, and cities — everything in it is imaginary. It's a novel, only a made up story. The dictionary says so and it's never wrong. Besides, everyone can go and do likewise. Shut your eyes. That's all that's necessary. There you have seen life from the other side.'

"That reminds me of the time when I was a little boy. I used to watch airplanes fly by in the sky and sometimes I'd stick my hands out to touch them. I was absolutely convinced that airplane was in the palm of my hand.

"I was a pretty strange kid."

MODERN ENGLISH

— Michael Conroy —   —Gary McDowell—
— Robbie Grey —

"How did we come up with the name Modern English? I think Richard, our drummer, originally thought of it. It seemed, at the time, there was something happening in England that wasn't happening anywhere else. People who didn't know what they were doing were getting together, forming bands and making noises, not necessarily musical noises either. It might have been happening everywhere else, but it just seemed to make more sense in England. Some people began to realize you could do more interesting stuff as well, rather than the punk thing where everything was so solid, y'know, like three chords and a violent scream over the top. It was a great adrenaline rush. You started to notice, not just yourself, that other bands were beginning to deviate and do different things. There seemed to be something happening that was completely 'English' and completely 'modern' as well.

"All the time we've been together we've never gone out of our way to please anyone except ourselves. That doesn't mean it's a bad thing to let audiences have a good time at concerts, but I do think there's a lot more to music than just playing. We like to think we haven't gone the same route that a lot of bands have, the ones who came out of the same era as we did, because now all they're doing is writing really banal lyrics. They may be writing well-structured pop songs, but I think they're more involved in it on the business side now. I want money, too, but I think if you can do it with a sense of style and install some pride in your work, when somebody asks you something, you'll be able to tell them the truth."
— Robbie Grey —

ORCHESTRAL MANOEUVRES in the DARK

— From left to right: Paul Humphreys, Andy McCluskey —

"When you grow up in a small suburb learning from mother and father and the local school. When you are in love with the possibilities of pop music and believe in the importance of writing songs of quality. Imagine the dilemma when — after spending years trying to achieve music of the quality you desired; after visiting places you had hardly believed that you could ever get to see; after being allowed a taste of that revered fame and that lusted-after money — what you learn from all your exertions is only the dubious nature of the values that led you to them in the first place."
— Andy McCluskey —

STEEL PULSE

— David Hinds —
— Phonso Martin —
— Ronald "Stepper" McQueen —

— Victor Yesufu —

— Selwyn "Bumbo" Brown —
— Steve "Grizzly" Nesbitt —

"There's a revolution of the senses happening at the moment, only this time it isn't physical, it's got to do with social change. I'm talking about black consciousness on a worldwide scale where you have a large concentration of black people in one area. Steel Pulse live in Birmingham, England, and it's predominantly made up of West Indian blacks and Asians. This consciousness brings the people closer together and it also gives them an awareness of where their culture is. You see, you're coming up to the second generation of black people in England — I'M TALKING ABOUT British-born black people whose parents originally came from Jamaica. Now is the time black rastas are being born and raised outside of their homeland. They're British but they're not looked upon as such because their culture is from another part of the world. The black man has to know more about his past. He has to come to terms where he's coming from. Marcus Garvey once said, 'A people without any knowledge of their history or an awareness of their culture is like a tree without its roots.'"

— Ronald "Stepper" McQueen —

JOHN COOPER CLARKE

"I memorize my poems by implementing a continuous fast-paced speed. It's an automatic mechanism. I usually switch into automatic because the whole thing of being on stage can be so potentially embarrassing. That's why I go to the extreme. Rapido is my thing. It's a way of getting it all out and making it less precious. I need rapido to remember the words. If I slow down I'm completely fucked. There isn't a formula for writing poetry. I wish there was. I've been looking for one. I think it's important to have a routine. I want to get an office eventually. I find it difficult to work at home, there's so many distractions. I want a routine because it concentrates your imagination, it doesn't destroy it. If you don't have a routine you'll never recognize what inspiration is when you get it because it's just part of your whole complicated life-style. I prefer to keep some sort of order over certain things. When I'm at home I'm obsessively neat. I'm Felix Unger of the Odd Couple."

NASH the SLASH

"The problem with the British audiences was that they didn't have a true perspective on what Nash the Slash was all about. The whole thing may have appeared to b a marvelous experience, but, in reality, the image and the characterization was regarded as a complete joke, a silly cabaret act. It's only the media and the record executives who misunderstand me. The public understands exactly what it is that I'm trying to do. I'm creating a theatrical image and I'm having a great deal of pleasure doing so. I've got fans that range between the ages of ten and seventy. It's interesting because they are the ones who can comprehend exactly what it is that I'm doing."

MEN WITHOUT HATS

— From left to right: Stefan Doroschuk, Colin Doroschuk, Allan McCarthy, Ivan —

"True, we may play electronics, but I like to look at it as if we're playing folk music. When Bob Dylan started out he played folk music. Look at people like Woody Guthrie and Bob Seger. Folk music is like a call to arms or 'We shall overcome' type of thing. When the guitar became popular it was the age of the troubadour, the poet-musician. Now everything has been reduced to micro chips. One person can have an orchestra at the touch of his or her fingertips. The synthesizer is the popular instrument of today. It's the folk instrument of the '80s. That's why there's been this rush of keyboard oriented bands. Technology has made it possible for a non-musician to make music. Brian Eno was the first person who made it legit for a non-musician to take a synthesizer and say, 'Hey, notes aren't the only thing. Sounds are something too. You don't have to know how to play the notes in order to make the sounds.' That turned a lot more people onto the actual manipulation of sound instead of picking up a guitar and trying to learn how to play it. Guitarists can tell if you're good or bad. They can pin down how many years you've been playing just by looking at you. But with a keyboard player, imagination is more than enough. If you have any amount of vision you can create virtually anything your little heart desires."

— Ivan —

A FLOCK of SEAGULLS

— From left to right: Paul Reynolds, Frank Maudsley, Mike Score, Ali Score —

"Technology frightens me, but, it was like when I was a kid spiders used to frighten me. I used to let them crawl all over me. It's a weird feeling to feel frightened and then have the thing that frightens you approach you before your very eyes. Technology is very similar because it tries to replace you but deep down inside you know it'll never happen. A sequencer can play a synthesizer better than I can but it'll never replace the excitement when I play it myself. Technology is here to be manipulated. Computors are here to do a job. Guitars and shoes have also been created to do a job. If you use them properly you can have a lot of fun with them. You can have a lot of fun with spiders as well. Did you know they go deaf when you pull their legs off? If you scare a spider into running away by trying to hit it, it'll run, but if you pull its legs off and hit it, chances are it won't run away."

— Mike Score —

LAURIE ANDERSON

"I don't have anything against virtuosity. I mean, I love going to concerts and hearing people play well. It's just not what I want to do, although I consider what I do extremely specific. It's not about vaguely making films and vaguely making tapes, but the point is to make a combination of things where you can receive all kinds of information at once stopping short of some kind of barrage so that it's not some sort of light show. My main fear in doing that, because a lot of my work has things to do with politics, economics and what's called 'the real world' as opposed to creating aesthetic situations, is the main pitfall, which is didacticism. If you use material that's that hot it's awfully easy to use that as a kind of forum for your own particular political or social ideas. I can't cut those things out but... That reminds me of the time when I was on a panel and some feminists were very angry at me for not being more specific about the woman's role.

"First of all, I think it's incredibly dangerous to work that way for two reasons, and one is that feminist ideas about the equality and ability of women, to my mind, are already beautiful and accurate. We don't have to dress and mock them up as art. Secondly, I think art is a very poor carrier of that kind of idea because it's not essentially fair. The difference between conveying an idea and conveying art is that art comes to you sensuously, it comes through your eyes and your ears. Ideas come straight into your brain, therefore, they're there to be analyzed and that's not primarily a sensuous experience. The best example I can think of is if you hear a song and it's the most beautiful song you've ever heard. You immediately love it but you can't quite understand the words. Eventually you hear it another fifty times and finally you understand the words and they're stupid words. You disagree with them. Suddenly they seem horrible but it's too late because you've already accepted the song, it's already inside you. If you present information like that you're not giving people a fair chance to evaluate it by saying, 'I don't agree with that,' or 'I agree with that.' The main thing I try to do is make the work open enough so that people can come into it and take what they want and leave what they don't want."

JAYNE COUNTY

"The treatment makes me feel good. It's a feeling I've always wanted. It's a need that's always been there ever since I can remember. When I was young boy I always wore women's clothes and all my friends were girls. I liked to play all the girls' games. I couldn't fit in with the boys at all. I didn't fit into that role. I didn't feel comfortable with it. It's just like my mother used to say, 'Since I was two or three I didn't want to play with the boys.' "

GUN CLUB

"A lot of time we'll play a Howlin' Wolf song, the same thing he wrote, but we just distort it, screw it up, mess it around, just add more of a feeling. It's like destroying what you like. I really love this music but I couldn't play it straight. I have to be more horrible about it. The standard blues isn't enough to satisfy me, although I can get real jazzed up, listening to a blues record. It's just an inception of a certain feeling, whereas by the time it gets to the band I'll already have advanced it three or four times until it's barely recognizable. It becomes much more negative. It's like taking the blues and turning it into suicide."

— Jeffrey Lee Pierce—

SHRIEKBACK

— From left to right: Dave Allen, Barry Andrews, Carl Marsh —

"What I'd like Shriekback to be is something that actually embraces what we're all about individually. For example, I'd like to go to Russia right now, and I could see how Shriekback could be a vehicle for us to do it. We found all the working relationships with our previous groups to have been very unsatisfying. Everyone tries to act democratic. They either have a discussion about what tracks should be included on the album or what the drums should sound like, but what's really going on is all this manipulation and politics between all the people involved. Nobody ever gets to talk about what's really going on. Everything becomes more and more ingrained and the people become more withdrawn. In the end all you're left with is all this covert hostility going under the guise of getting the job done, and it's not very satisfying to work that way. Shriekback are committed to not working that way. You see, Shriekback can be whatever we want it to be. It isn't so much that it's a thing within a structure, but it is a structure in itself. Instead of having a group as something that you do, as opposed to something else you do, it's as much a tool and a structure for achieving other things as well."

— Barry Andrews —

ROMEO VOID

"The thing about anybody ever writing about you is that it's always what they think, it's never what you think. But I've had the greatest time with the review of the Benefactor LP in Rolling Stone, which implies that the song Never Say Never is about my father and the Oedipus complex and la de da. For one thing the guy doesn't know his Greek, it's Electra complex, not Oedipus, and also that he's approaching it from a real Freudian point of view, which is not a very modern way of thinking at all. It's more Jungian — 'Nursing the father locked inside him,' anima-animus, the varied sexism inside your own psyche. Also his fascination with sexual imagery is typical of a male voyeur attitude, rather than, of course, how I'm writing it which is as an engaged person. All he can see is his own little fantasy. (laughter) People come up to me at concerts all the time now and ask me if Never Say Never is about my father. No! And then he went on about the man in SOS being my father, but it's like, I'm sorry, in SOS I never say it's a man. I speak first and third person in the same song. Put 'em outside, put 'em inside, put 'em outside, put 'em inside, see it in someone else, see it in yourself. There's a lyric from the song Orange which reads, 'I have a friend. It moves me.' So what does the reviewer say? He asks if the song's about masturbation. Another lyric in the song reads, 'His eyes are a beautiful grey, he wanted to go away. I said stay, stay.' Wait a minute, that's not about masturbation!"

— Debora Iyall —

STRANGLERS

"Why do you end up doing what you do? How much control do you have over it? Do you want control over it? If you do want control over it, how will you know when you have it? How much of it is luck? Does luck actually exist? These are just some of the things I've learned about life and the fact that luck and fate don't really exist, but, in fact, they do.

"George Melly [a British surrealist/writer] once told me, 'If you meet someone twice by accident you know that you're going to bump into them a third time without question.' Is that fate or coincidence? People say, 'Yeah, I'm a product of my environment, man. I've got no control.' You have to remember that your environment is a product of you as well. How many times have you been thinking about someone and then you've met them or they've phoned you. Is it a coincidence? I think there's a lot more to it than that. In fact, I think you can direct it just by being intuitive. What first appears to be a major happening, can, in fact, be very significant. I think people are given these signals throughout their lives but they rarely pay any attention to them. That's why most of them end up leading very unfulfilled, frustrating lives."

— Hugh Cornwell —

RED DECADE

"I use the word 'composer' because it has nothing to do with being a musician. A composer usually makes a decision to put his or her idea down on paper. Musicians are usually more talented players who often have more ideas. The only drawback is that they have great difficulty talking to me with their instruments. Maybe this makes me out to be a closet romantic. It's got no relation to the British term 'New Romantic,' thank god. When I see a New Romantic band I automatically think of three guys who got together, bought out all the old clothes in London and decided to re-sell them. It's making electronic music very palatable, but most of the people who are doing it don't have any imagination.

"You're talking about selling your imagination. You're talking about convincing the world that your imagination is viable and that just by expressing it you should be fed, housed and given a generous supply of drugs. Is that what musicians are concerned about? I don't think they've decided what they're saying is valid. I have. I'm a composer."

— Jules Baptiste —

U2

— From left to right: Bono, The Edge, Larry Mullen, Adam Clayton —

"I realize coming from Ireland and all, we should be writing about the troubles of the civil war, but I don't think our songs would mean as much if we wrote what everyone expected us to instead of writing about what we think is important. Besides, there are more bombings in London connected with troubles than there are in Dublin. I mean, Dublin is relatively quiet, and musically it's considered to be something of a backwater. We live in an area called The Village, and that's where we got our names. For instance, I was given the name 'Edge' because my face has many angles. It's how we do things there. Maybe people don't understand it yet. They will."

— The Edge —

LEISURE PROCESS

— From left to right: Gary Barnacle, Ross Middleton —

"I thrive on hatred. If I'm in a club and there's a lot of other people from other bands there and they're sneering and not talking to me, I thrive on it. It's like a real liquor or something. You sip it down. You just think about all these people standing there and saying, 'I fucking hate Leisure Process,' and that's great. I feed off that. But if there's a bunch of people who don't even want to know you, it's terrible. Leisure Process demands love or hate. We don't want anything in-between. I don't want people saying, 'Oh that's quite a nice record.' I hope people like that die. This is the Nick Cave/Birthday Party impersonation — 'I HOPE PEOPLE ARE GONNA DIE!!!' I like the Birthday Party. They're brilliant. I bet they hate Leisure Process though. Nick Cave would probably say, 'I spit on Leisure Process's grave,' but I don't give a flying fuck. I think they're great.

"What pop has meant to me is things like Napoleon Solo's suits and Marc Bolan actually 'getting on' Top Of The Pops with Get It On, which was wonderful. Most of the current things don't even come from music. Pop is just an episode of 'Coronation Street.' You're absorbed for thirty minutes. It's not a great art form. It's not even that meaningful. It gives people a lot of pleasure though. Paul Morley defined it really well when he interviewed Pete Townshend several months ago. He thought pop music was a series of constant attempts at telling people the truth, and I think I'd have to agree with him. Nobody has to go into the studio and make a record, but something pushes you to do it. It's got nothing to do with becoming a star or making lots of money. That's peripheral. That comes later, if you're lucky. Pop is about the urge to make pop records. God knows what that's about. It's not simple, but I never said it was a simple business."

— Ross Middleton —

A SELECTED DISCOGRAPHY

King Sunny Adé p. 107
Adé was born into a royal family in his native Ondo, a Yoruba town in western Nigeria, and is currently hailed as the reigning king of juju music. In 1966 Sunny formed his first group which consisted of eight musicians. Today King Sunny Adé and his African Beats have increased their membership to a modest twenty. Adé and his African Beats combine traditional Nigerian juju music with the latest in electric instruments. Since he started his career 17 years ago, Adé has recorded close to 45 albums. King Sunny Adé is the most important pop figure to emerge from the international music scene in the last 15 years.
Origin: Nigerian
Labels: *African Artist **Sonny Alede †Island
Top L.P.'s: *Chapter 1 (1971), *Searching For My Love (1975), **Festac '77 (1977), *365 Is My Number (1978), **The Message (1980), **Maajo (1981), †Ju Ju Music (1982), †Synchro System (1983).
Recent Singles: †Jafummi/Instrumental (1981), †Ma Jaiye Oni/The Message (1982), †Synchro System/Ire (1983).

Afrika Bambaataa p. 41
What does the name Afrika Bambaataa mean? "The name comes from the Zulu nation of South Africa," explains Bambaataa. "It was the name of a Zulu chief who was born in 1865, if I'm not mistaken, and he died in 1906. He was one of the last great kings to fight against the British to keep his country free from being taken over. It means affectionate leader."
Origin: American
Label: Tommy Boy
12" E.P.'s: Planet Rock / Instrumental mix (1982), Looking For The Perfect Beat / Instrumental mix (1983).

Laurie Anderson p. 128
Laurie originally launched her career as sculptor. Eventually she began toying with electronic modulations, voice, spoken words, violin, tapes and slide projections. This year Laurie will be releasing her follow-up album to *Big Science*. It will also be available as a video disc through Warner Communications.
Origin: American
Lables: *One Ten **Giorno Poetry Systems †Warner Brothers
Top L.P.'s: **You're The Guy I Want To Share My Money With, featuring John Giorno and William Burroughs (1981), †Big Science (1982).
Pick Singles: *O Superman / Walk The Dog (1981 — re-release on Warners in the same year), †Big Science / Example #22 (1982), It's Not The Bullet That Kills You, It's The Hole (Holly Solomon Gallery Editions 004 Ltd. Editions of 500 — 1977), Let X = X (flexi-disc in Artforum Magazine — 1981).

APB p. 88
This exuberant four-piece funkaholic band hails from Aberdeenshire, Scotland. Over the past two years they've released four impressive singles in the U.K.; however, it was their second one, *Shoot You Down*, that caught on as a favorite in the New York dance clubs. APB headlined at N.Y.'s prestigious club, the Ritz, this past April of '83.
  Iain Slater, lead vocals, bass; *Nick Jones*, percussion; *George Cheyne*, drums; *Glenn Roberts*, guitar.
Origin: Scottish
Label: Oily
Top L.P.: Debut L.P. due soon (worldwide).
Pick Singles: Chain Reaction / Power Crisis (1981), Shoot You Down / Talk To Me (1981), Palace Filled With Love / All Your Life With Me (1982), Rainy Day / From You And Back To You (1982), One Day / Help Yourself — forthcoming single on new label (1983).

Bad Brains p. 82
Bad Brains is a former jazz/funk fusion group from Washington D.C., who, in 1977, lifted their name from a Ramones' song title, and after hearing other punk rockers such as the Dead Boys, slowly realized they had something in common — rebellion. The Brains, also inspired by the great king of reggae, Bob Marley, began to build a connection with the Rastafari way of knowledge and the praising of Jah. For the first time here is an American black group who played the best of both musics — hardcore punk and reggae.
  H.R. vocals; *Darryl Jenifer*, bass; *Earl Hudson*, drums; *Dr. Know*, guitar.
Origin: American
Labels: *Bad Brains **Alternative Tentacles †Passport
Top L.P.: †Rock For Light (1983)
Pick Singles: *Pay To Cum / Stay Close To Me (1980), **12" E.P., Bad Brains featuring I Luv I Jah, I, Sailin' On and Big Takeover (1981), *12" E.P., I & I Survive Destroy Babylon / Coptic Times / Joshua's Son (1982).

Bauhaus p. 13
The name "Bauhaus" was adapted from the reknowned Weimar Republic School of Design from the 1920s. As a pop group, Bauhaus are something of an experimental institution in their own right. In 1981, bassist David Jay recorded the single *Nothing/Armour* with the 81-year-old painter, writer, and lecturer, Rene Halket, one of the few surviving members of the original 1923 workshop, "Staatliches Bauhaus Weimar." Guitarist Daniel Ash has also pursued solo projects including three 12" E.P.'s recorded with multi-instrumentalist Glenn Campling

under the name "Tones On Tail." Although they've been hailed as a glam rock band, Bauhaus isn't trying to resurrect the early '70s makeup/slash glitter of Marc Bolan and David Bowie. True, recording a rendition of Bowie's *Ziggy Stardust* in '82 didn't help to demystify the controversy, it only strengthened it.

David Jay, bass, piano; *Kevin Haskins*, drums; *Peter Murphy*, lead vocals; *Daniel Ash*, guitar, vocals.

Origin:	British
Labels:	*Small Wonder **4.A.D. †Beggars Banquet
Top L.P.'s:	†*In The Flat Field* (1980), †*Mask* (1981), †*The Sky's Gone Out* (1982).
Pick Singles:	**Bela Lugosi's Dead*, 12" (1979), ***Dark Entries / Untitled* (1980), ***Telegram Sam / Crowds* (1980), †*Kick In The Eye / Satori* (1981), †*The Passion Of Lovers / Jay, Murphy, Haskins & Ash* (1981), †*Spirit / Terror Couple "Live"* (1982), †*Lagartija Nick / Paranoia, Paranoia* (1983), †*She's In Parties / Departures* (1983).

The Belle Stars   p. 78

At one time four out of seven of these musicians played for the 2-Tone label all-girl group, the Bodysnatchers. You may remember their hit *Do The Rock Steady*. The ska-influenced beat group eventually split up in October 1980 and rhythm guitarist Stella Barker, lead guitarist Sara-Jane Owen, saxophonist Miranda Joyce, and drummer Judy Parsons went on to form a brand new group — the Belle Stars. After auditioning for a vocalist, the band recruited Jennie McKeown. The British-based Belle Stars finally scored a Top Ten single in 1983 with *Sign Of The Times*.

Stella Barker, guitar; *Jennie McKeown*, lead vocals; *Judy Parsons*, drums; *Lesley Shone*, bass; *Miranda Joyce*, sax; *Sarah-Jane Owen*, lead guitar, vocals; *Clare Hirst*, sax.

Origin:	British
Label:	Stiff
Top L.P.:	*The Belle Stars* (1983).
Pick Singles:	*Hiawatha / Big Blonde* (1981), *Slick Trick / Take Another Look* (1981), *Another Latin Love Song / Miss World / Stop Now / Having A Good Time* (1981), *Iko Iko / The Reason* (1982), *The Clapping Song / Blame* (1982), *Mockingbird / Turn Back The Clock* (1982), *Sign Of The Times / Madness* (1983), *Sweet Memory / April Fool* (1983).

Big Country   p. 71

Big Country revitalized the British pop charts this past April when their single *Fields Of Fire* climbed into the Top Ten. You may remember Stuart Adamson, former guitarist for the now defunct Scottish-based pop group The Skids. This time around Adamson sings lead vocals as well as playing guitar. And yet, it is Big Country's rhythm section, bassist Tony Butler and drummer Mark Brzezicki who give the sound its distinctive edge. Bruce Watson, the second Scottish member of Big Country, rounds out the group's heroic sound with some downright adventurous guitar playing.

Stuart Adamson, lead vocals, guitar; *Tony Butler*, bass, vocals; *Bruce Watson*, guitar, vocals; *Mark Brzezicki*, drums.

Origin:	Scottish/British
Label:	Phonogram
Top L.P.:	Debut L.P. soon to be released.
Pick Singles:	*Harvest Home / Balcony* (1982), *Fields Of Fire / Angle Park* (1983).

The Birthday Party   p. 101

Originally called The Boys Next Door in '78, The Birthday Party eventually moved from their native Melbourne, Australia to London, England to make it in popular music. Their sound is unaffected, demonic and very stimulating. At its best it is often distorted, nightmarish and deliciously crude. They just recently signed a recording contract with Mute Records.

Rowland S. Howard, guitar; *Nick Cave*, vocals; *Tracy Pew*, bass; *Mick Harvey*, drums.

Origin:	Australian
Labels:	*Suicide **Missing Link †4.A.D.
Top L.P.'s:	**Lethal Weapons*, an Australian punk rock compilation featuring the Boys Next Door tracks *Shivers, Boy Hero* and *Masturbation Generation* (1978), ***Door Door* (1978), ***Hee-Haw*, 12" E.P. (1979), †*Prayers On Fire* (1981), †*Junkyard* (1982), †*Bad Seed*, 12" E.P. (1983).
Pick Singles:	†*Mr. Clarinet / Happy Birthday* (1979), †*Friend Catcher / Waving My Arms* (1980), †*Drunk On The Pope's Blood*, 12" E.P. (1981), †*Release The Bats / Blast Off* (1981).

Blancmange   p. 112

Blancmange is an unlikely name for an electronic pop duo. In Britain the name is derived from a popular flavored gelatin powder, something like a cross between a jello mold and pudding. Synthesist Stephen Luscombe and vocalist Neil Arthur openly admit that they lift anything they can get their hands on whether it be instruments or influences. They refuse to pin themselves down. Their sound is luscious with its monster percussive beat and repetitive synthe rhythms.

Neil Arthur, vocals, guitar, electronics; *Stephen Luscombe*, synthesizers, keyboards.

Origin:	British
Label:	London
Top L.P.:	*Happy Families* (1982).
Pick Singles:	*God's Kitchen / I've Seen The Word* (1982), *Feel Me / Instrumental* (1982), *Living On The Ceiling*, 12" (1982), *Waves*, 12" E.P. featuring *Business Steps* and *The Game Above My Head* (1983), *Blind Vision / Heaven Knows Where Heaven Is / On Our Way To?* — music excerpt from the

film "Duet", 12" E.P. (1983).

The Blasters p. 76
Jeffery Lee Pierce of the Gun Club once said the best rockabilly band he ever heard were the Blasters from California. But they combine several different styles of American music — R&B, blues, jazz, hillbilly, be-bop, rock'n'roll and swing.

Phil Alvin, vocals, guitar, harmonica; *Dave Alvin*, lead guitar; *John Bazz*, bass, *Bill Bateman*, drums; *Gene Taylor*, piano; *Lee Allen*, sax; *Steve Berlin*, sax.

Origin:	*American*
Label:	*Slash*
Top L.P.'s:	*The Blasters* (1981), *Over There, Live At The Venue*, 12" E.P. featuring *High School Confidential, Rock Boppin' Baby, Keep A Knockin', I Don't Want To, Go, Go, Go* and *Roll 'Em Pete* (1982), *Non-Fiction* (1983).
Pick Singles:	*I'm Shakin' / No Other Girl* (1982), *So Long Baby, Goodbye / Border Radio* (1982), *Barefoot Rock*, 12" E.P. featuring *Fool's Paradise* and *Long White Cadillac*.

Bow Wow Wow p. 52
The musicians in this particular group used to be the original members of Adam and the Ants. Drummer Dave Barbarossa, guitarist Matthew Ashman and bassist Leroy Gorman were responsible for popularizing the burundi drum pop sound. Out of all the latest in British groups, Bow Wow Wow are one of the very few who have actually captured the essence of pop at its most imaginative.

Dave Barbarossa, drums; *Annabella Lwin*, vocals; *Leroy Gorman*, bass; *Matthew Ashman*, guitar.

Origin:	*British*
Labels:	**EMI **RCA*
Top L.P.'s:	***See Jungle! See Jungle! Go Join Your Gang Yeah! City All Over, Go Ape Crazy* (1981), ***I Want Candy* (1982), **Original Recordings* (1982), ***When The Going Gets Tough, The Tough Gets Going* (1983).
Pick Singles:	**C'30 C'60 C'90 GO! / Sun, Sea And Piracy* (1980), **Work / C'30 C'60 C'90 Anda!* (1980), ***Chihuahua / Golly! Golly! Go Buddy!* (1981), ***Go Wild In The Country / El Boss Dicho!* (1981), ***Jungle Boy / T.V. Savage* (1982), ***I Want Candy / Elimination Dancing* (1982), ***Do You Wanna Hold Me? / What's The Time (Hey Buddy)* (1983).

Glenn Branca p. 16
Glenn Branca could very well be hailed as New York City's foremost avant-garde manipulator of the contemporary electric guitar. Branca, along with fellow sound experimentalists like Rhys Chatham, David Van Tieghem, Ned Sublette, Jules Baptiste and Laurie Anderson, are the modern-day equivalents to the pioneers of sound introspection — John Cage, Steve Reich, Stockhausen, Robert Ashley and Phillip Glass.

Guitars: *Glenn Branca, Thurston Moore, Lee Ranaldo, David Rosenbloom, Ned Sublette*; Bass: *Jeffrey Glenn*; Drums, *Stephen Wischerth*.

Origin:	*American*
Labels:	**99 **Giorno Poetry Systems †Neutral*
Recordings:	**Lesson No. 1 / Dissonance* (1980), **The Ascension* (debut L.P., 1981), ***Who You Staring At? Glenn Branca and John Giorno*. Side 1 features music by Branca for the dance *Bad Smells*, choreographed by Twyla Tharp (1982), *†Symphony No. 4 (Gloria)* (1983).

Breeding Ground p. 92
Breeding Ground moved from Ottawa to Toronto and are one of the few independent recording artists to strike up a following in new music circles. The strong theatrical presence of John Shirreff at live shows is worth seeing.

Ken Jones, drums, percussion; *Jonathan Strayer*, bass, vocals; *Hugh Gladish*, guitar, vocals; *John Shirreff*, lead vocals, shirts.

Origin:	*Canadian*
Label:	*Mannequin*
Top L.P.:	*Breeding Ground*, 4-song E.P. featuring *Wintergarden, Dirge, Thin Red Line* and *Underground*.
Pick Singles:	*Reunion / Slaughter* (soon to be released 12" mix).

Bush Tetras p. 25
Slide guitarist Pat Place originally played with James Chance and the Contortions, and maybe that's why you might pick up on her unique "flaming licks" in the Tetras' music. Original bassist Laura Kennedy left the group during the latter part of 1982. Her current replacement is Bobbie Albertson, formerly of the Outsets. Drummer Dee Pop also split from the group, only to be replaced by Donnie Christensen, formerly of the Contortions and the Raybeats.

Cynthia Sley, vocals; *Pat Place*, guitar; *Bobbie Albertson*, bass; *Donnie Christensen*, drums.

Origin:	*American*
Labels:	**99 **Fetish †Stiff America ††Stiff U.K.*
Top L.P.'s:	*††Start Swimming*, "Live" compilation featuring 2 Tetras' tracks *Cold Turkey* and *Punch Drunk* (1981), *†**Rituals*, 12" E.P. (1981).
Pick Singles:	**Too Many Creeps / Snakes Crawl / You Taste Like The Tropics* (1980), ***Boom / Das Ah Riot* (1981).
Cassette:	*Wild Things*, "Live" (1983). Available on ROIR cassettes.

David Byrne   p. 21

The interesting thing about David Byrne is his uncanny sense of creativity. He's constantly working on new projects whether it be soundtracks for dance productions, video tapes, album productions (including the B 52's and Funboy Three) or the Talking Heads.

Origin:	American
Label:	Sire
Top L.P.'s:	*Talking Heads '77* (1977), *More Songs About Buildings & Food* (1978), *Fear Of Music* (1979), *Remain In Light* (1980), *My Life In The Bush Of Ghosts* (1981), *The Catherine Wheel* (1981), *The Name Of This Band Is Talking Heads* (1982), *Speaking In Tongues* (1983).
Pick Singles:	*Love Goes To A Building On Fire / New Feeling* (1977), *Psycho Killer / Psycho Killer* (acoustic) (1977), *Take Me To The River / Thank You For Sending Me An Angel* (1978), *Life During Wartime / Electric Guitar* (1979), *Once In A Lifetime / Seen And Not Seen* (1980), *Houses In Motion / Air* (1981), *The Jezebel Spirit / Regiment / Very Very Hungry*, 12" (1981), *Big Blue Plymouth / Leg Bells* (1981).

John Cale   p. 105

This man is such an influential force for everybody who first discovered him in the Velvet Underground in the mid '60s. His production credits include Iggy and the Stooges, Nico and Squeeze.

Origin:	British
Labels:	*Reprise **CBS †Island ††Illegal/I.R.S. ‡A&M ‡‡Ze
Top Solo L.P.'s:	**Church Of Anthrax* (1970), **The Academy In Peril* (1972), **Paris 1919* (1973), †*Fear* (1974), †*Slow Dazzle* (1975), †*Helen Of Troy* (1975), ††*Animal Justice, E.P.* featuring *Chicken Shit / Memphis / Tin Pan Punk / Hedda Gabbler* (1977), ‡*Sabotage "Live"* (1979), ‡*Honi Soit* (1981), ‡‡*Music For A New Society* (1982).

Jim Carroll   p. 111

At 16 years of age Carroll published his first book of prose, *The Basketball Diaries*, an autobiographical account about life on the streets of New York. At 22 he published his second book *Living At The Movies*. Carroll ended up reciting some of his poetry at a Patti Smith concert, of all places. Since then, Carroll's been entertaining rock audiences as well as holding readings in the poetry circles. In 1982 he starred in Ron Mann's perceptive documentary *Poetry In Motion*.

Origin:	American
Labels:	*Atco **Giorno Poetry Systems
Top L.P.'s:	*Catholic Boy* (1980), *Dry Dreams* (1982), **Life Is A Killer* featuring *Just Visiting* from Carroll's forthcoming book *The Book Of Nods* (1983).
Pick Singles:	*People Who Died / I Want The Angel* (1980), *Day and Night / Wicked Gravity* (1980).

Rhys Chatham   p. 38

Chatham is an astounding avant-garde electric guitarist/composer currently living in New York City. He founded the music programme at The Kitchen (N.Y.C.'s first ever performance arts centre). He's already spent two terms at The Kitchen as musical director — 1971-1973, 1977-1980. He's performed with such notable experimentalists as Glenn Branca, Peter Gordon, Jules Baptiste, Laurie Anderson and Robert Ashley. Chatham is currently recording tracks for an upcoming E.P. which will be available on Lovely Music Records sometime in 1983.

Origin:	American
Rare Recordings:	*Excerpt From 64 Short Stories* Rhys Chatham with David Lynton (Just Another Asshole Mag. No. 5 — 1981), *Drastic Classical Music For Electronic Instruments* (Antartica Records — 1982).

John Cooper Clarke   p. 124

This is Britain's coolest and most controversial poet in pop. At 12 years of age, when he was growing up in Manchester, Clarke had a longing desire to become a famous crime novelist. In his lean teen years he played in two underground psychedelic groups, the Ferrets and the Curious Yellows. His first serious gig for reciting his poetry was at a striptease club in Manchester called the *New Luxor*. He initially got signed to Epic Records after he'd been on tour with the Buzzcocks in '77, opening shows and building up a strong punk following. Now, his prose is accompanied with tasteful electronics supplied by Martin Hannett's Invisible Girls. He recently had his first book published titled TEN YEARS IN AN OPEN-NECKED SHIRT.

Origin:	British
Labels:	*Rabid **Epic
Top L.P.'s:	**Love In Disguise* (1978), **Walking Back To Happiness*, 10" "live" E.P. (1979), **Snap, Crackle and Bop* (1980), **Zip Style Method* (1982).
Pick Singles:	*Innocents / Suspended Sentence / Psycle Sluts* (1977), **Post War Glamour Girl / Kung Fu International* (1978), **Gimmix / I Married A Monster From Outer Space* (1979), **Splat Twat / Sleepwalk* (1979), **It Man / Thirty Six Hours* (1980), **The Day My Pad Went Mad / A Distant Relation* (1982), **Night People / The Face Behind The Scream* (1982).

Julian Cope p. 110

"What I do is more confusing," offers Julian Cope, former singer/songwriter for the now defunct Teardrop Explodes. "I never try to make any provocative statements." Teardrop made their first public appearance at *Eric's*, a popular Liverpool club, during November of '78. Cope's previous music experience included a brief stint with The Crucial Three, a three-piece that also featured Ian (Bunnymen) McCulloch and Pete (Wah!) Wylie. Some of the outside projects Cope pursued when he was with Teardrop included a compilation album that he put together of the late '60s British psychedelic singer, Scott Walker, and he also opened *Club Zoo*, his very own club in Liverpool. At the moment he's recording new material for a forthcoming solo single entitled *Strasbourg* and an album.

Origin: *British*
Labels: *Zoo **Mercury / Phonogram
Top L.P.'s: **Kilimanjaro (1980), **Wilder (1981).
Pick Singles: *Bouncing Babies / All I Am Is Loving You (1979), **Treason / Read It In Books (1980), **Reward / Strange House In The Snow (1981), **Passionate Friend / Christ vs. Warhol (1981), **Tiny Children / Rachael Built A Steamboat (1982), **You Disappear From View / Suffocate (1983).

Jayne County p. 129

With the exception of Amanda Leer, Jayne County is the first pop performer to have undergone a sex change. You may remember her previous groups, The Backstreet Boys, and The Electric Chairs. As Wayne, Jayne got interested in gospel music when she was a young boy growing up in America's deep south. At the age of 17, Wayne moved to Atlanta, and started entertaining clubs as a female impersonator, recreating the likes of Cher, Janis Joplin, and Dusty Springfield. Next stop: New York, where County got involved in the underground theatre scene, Andy Warhol and rock'n'roll.

Origin: *American*
Labels: *Max **Safari †Illegal ††Attic
Top L.P.'s: **Blatantly Offensive (1978), **Storm The Gates Of Heaven (1978), **Man Enough To Be A Woman (1978), **Things Your Mother Never Told You (1979), ††Rock'n'Roll Resurrection (1980).
Pick Singles: *Max's Kansas City Pts. 1&2 (1976), **Blatantly Offensive E.P. featuring Fuck Off, Mean Mutherfuckin' Man and Toilet Love (1977), †Stuck On You / Paranoia Paradise / The Last Time (1977), †Thunder When She Walks / What You Got (1977), **Eddie & Sheena / Rock'n'Roll Cleopatra (1978), **Trying To Get On The Radio / Evil Minded Mamma (1978), **Berlin / Waiting For The Marines (1978), **So Many Ways / J'Attends Les Marines (1979).

The Cramps p. 15

Throughout their colourful eight years together, the Cramps have never had a bass player. They prefer to use two guitars. Their inspiration stems from various rock eras including psychedelia, surf, instrumental rock anthems (movie soundtracks) and vintage '60s punk. Original guitarist Bryan Gregory left the band several years ago. His current replacement is Kid Congo, a native of L.A. who used to play with Jeffrey Lee Pierce of the Gun Club.

Nick Knox, drums; *Ivy Rorschach*, guitar; *Kid Congo*, guitar; *Lux Interior*, lead vocals.

Origin: *American*
Label: *Vengeance **Illegal / I.R.S.
Top L.P.'s: **Gravest Hits E.P. (1979), **Songs The Lord Taught Us (1979), **Psychedelic Jungle (1980).
Pick Singles: *Surfin' Bird / The Way I Walk (1977), *Human Fly / Domino (1978), **Fever / Garbageman (1980), **Drug Train / Love Me / I Can't Hardly Stand It (1980), **Goo Goo Muck / She Said (1980), **The Crusher / Save It / New Kind Of Kick, 12" (1980).

Cristina p. 57

Cristina developed a strong interest in theatre. She attended the Central School of Drama in Britain, and eventually went on to study French and English literature at Harvard University in Cambridge, Massachusetts. Her debut single, *Disco Clone* (produced by John Cale in '78) came out from an infatuation that she had with Bertolt Brecht's "Threepenny Opera". You may remember her for her sado-masochistic send-up of the Leiber/Stroller classic *Is That All There Is?* The single was released in Britain in '79. Her debut album *Cristina* was, interestingly enough, written and produced by August Darnell of Kid Creole & the Coconuts. Her latest L.P. *Sleep It Off* features lyrics written by Cristina herself, while the music and production is handled by Don Was of "Was Not Was" fame.

Origin: *American*
Labels: *Ze **Polydor
Top L.P.'s: *Cristina (1979), *A Christmas Record (1981), **Sleep It Off (1983).
Pick Singles: *Disco Clone / "French version" (1978), *Is That All There Is? / Jungle Love (1979), *Drive My Car / Don't Be Greedy (1979), *Things Fall Apart / Ballad Of Immoral Manufacture (1981).

Culture Club p. 36

One of the few commercially successful groups of last year who actually proved they could recreate their music in an exciting live fashion. Their sound echoes an array of musics ranging from reggae, funk, calypso, rumba, to Motown and pop à la Burt Bacharach. Culture Club's music is positive and joyous, a call to all ethnic backgrounds to celebrate life, which accounts for the band's popularity.

Jon Moss, drums; *Michael Craig*, bass; *Roy Hay*, guitar; *Boy George*, vocals.

Origin: British
Label: Virgin
Top L.P.: *Kissing To Be Clever* (1982).
Pick Singles: *White Boy / Love Twist* (1982), *I'm Afraid Of Me / Murder Rap Trap* (1982), *Do You Really Want To Hurt Me? / Love Is Cold* (1982), *Time (Clock Of The Heart) / White Boys Can't Control It* (1982), *Church Of The Poison Mind / Man Shake* (1983).

The Cure   p. 70

At the moment the future of the group is a mystery. Vocalist/guitarist Robert Smith is presently playing guitar for Siouxsie and the Banshees. Recently bassist Simon Gallup joined former Cure keyboardist Matthieu Hartley to form a new group entitled Cry. Judging from the Cure's most recent single, *Let's Go To Bed*, their sound is leaning towards a predominantly electronic dance feel, considerably more uptempo than their previous efforts.

Lol Tolhurst, drums, percussion, electronics; *Robert Smith*, vocals, guitar, keyboards.

Origin: British
Labels: *Small Wonder **Fiction
Top L.P.'s: **Three Imaginary Boys* (1979), **Seventeen Seconds* (1980), **Faith* (1981), **Pornography* (1982).
Pick Singles: *Killing An Arab / 10:15 Saturday Night* (1978), **Boys Don't Cry / Plastic Passion* (1979) **Jumping Someone Else's Train / I'm Cold* (1979), **A Forest / Another Journey By Train* (1980), **Primary / Descent* (1981), **Charlotte Sometimes / Splintered In Her Head* (1981), **Hanging Garden / One Hundred Years* (1982), **Let's Go To Bed / Just One Kiss* (1982).

Dead Kennedys   p. 106

Have you ever had the unexpected pleasure of attending a Dead Kennedy's concert? For some reason or another, people like to climb onto the stage, grab the microphone, shout an obscenity into it, and then they dive headfirst into the crowd below. In 1980 Biafra ran a campaign for mayor of San Francisco. He received 6,591 votes. Not bad.

Jello Biafra, vocals; *Klaus Flouride*, bass; *D.H. Peligro* and *East Bay Ray*, guitars.

Origin: American
Label: Alternative Tentacles
Top L.P.'s: *Fresh Fruit For Rotting Vegetables* (1980), *In God We Trust Inc.* (1981), *Plastic Surgery Disasters* (1982).
Pick Singles: *California Umbrellas / Man With The Dogs* (1979), *Holiday In Cambodia / Police Truck* (1980), *Too Drunk To Fuck / The Prey* (1981), *Nazi Punks Fuck Off / Moral Majority* (1981), *Halloween / Saturday Night Holocaust* (1982).

Defunkt   p. 35

Trombonist/vocalist Joe Bowie is always determined to develop his brand of polyrhythmic funk to new heights. The sound is urban and African, each instrument playing its own distinctive rhythm. This is what gives the overall sound its multi-layered effect. The group's third effort *Thermo Nuclear Sweat* actually pushes the limits of progressive funk without being repetitive or mundane (like most white crossover funk groups).

Joe Bowie, trombone, vocals; *John Mulkerin*, trumpet; *Kelvyn Bell*, guitar; *Kim Clarke*, bass; *Kenny Martin*, drums.

Origin: American
Label: Hannibal
Top L.P.'s: *Defunkt* (1980), 12" E.P. *Razor's Edge, Stranglin' Me With Your Love "Revisited"* (1981), *Thermo Nuclear Sweat* (1982).

Gabi Delgado   p. 54

Dusseldorf-based D.A.F. paved the way for a new kind of European electronic jive. Now, since their amicable split in 1982, D.A.F. members drummer Robert Gorl and vocalist Gabi Delgado have gone their separate ways. Delgado's new solo album on the Virgin label is entitled *Mistress*. It's a brave attempt at combining South American music, cosmopolitan funk and free-form jazz. This time around Delgado made his mind up to drop German, and is currently singing in English and Spanish.

Origin: Spanish
Labels: *Mute **Virgin
Top L.P.'s: *Die Kleinen Und Die Bosen* (1980), **Alles Ist Gut* (1981), **Gold Und Liebe* (1981), **Fur Immer* (1982), **Mistress* (recorded in two versions — Spanish and English) (1983).
Pick Singles: *Kebabtraume / Gewalt* (1980), *Der Rauber Und Der Prinz / Tanz Mit Mir* (1980), **Der Mussolini / Der Rauber Und Der Prinz* (1981), **Goldenes Spielzeug (Gold Gold Gold) / El Que*, 12" (1981), **Sex Unter Wasser / Knocken Auf Knochen* (1981), **Verlieb Dich In Mich / Ein Bisschen Kreig*, 12" (1982), **History Of A Kiss / Sex Goddess* (1983).

Howard Devoto   p. 75

Originally vocalist for the now defunct, Manchester-based Buzzcocks, Howard Devoto recorded *Spiral Scratch*, probably Britain's all-time quintessential punk E.P. (Dec. '76). Come '77, Devoto left the Buzzcocks to form Magazine, yet another group who went on to record their debut single in early '78 — *Shot By Both Sides*. Magazine disbanded in '81. After two years of silence, Devoto developed a rapport with Bernard Szajner, a French audio visual technician turned electronic composer. Devoto was asked to write lyrics to three of Szajner's pieces — *Without Living, The Convention* and

Deal of the Century. Upon completion, Devoto flew to Paris to sing the lyrics on Szajner's *Brute Reason* L.P., and, in turn, performed with the composer on a national tour of France which eventually brought the two to London during May '83. Interestingly enough, Devoto will commence his very own tour of England when his long awaited solo album is released this June.

Origin:	*British*
Labels:	**New Hormones* ***Virgin*
Top L.P.'s:	***Real Life (1978),*** ***Secondhand Daylight (1979),*** ***The Correct Use Of Soap (1980),*** ***Play (1980), **Magic, Murder and the Weather (1981), Brute Reason,*** Szajner's new album on Island Records. Howard is featured on three of the tracks, (1983). A forthcoming solo album will be issued in June on Virgin.
Pick Singles:	**Spiral Scratch, 7" E.P. (1977),* ***Shot By Both Sides / My Mind Ain't So Open (1978), **Rhythm Of Cruelty / T.V. Baby (1979),*** ***Give Me Everything / I Love You You Big Dummy (1978), **A Song From Under The Floorboards / Twenty Years Ago (1980), **Thank You (Falettinme Be Mice Elf Agin) / The Book (1980), **About The Weather / In The Dark (1981),*** ***Rainy Season / Rain Forest (1983).***

Thomas Dolby   p. 67

Dolby is a solo singer/songwriter and synthesist whose one-man stageshow combines electronics, slide, and film projections and video. In 1981, during the recording of his debut album *The Golden Age Of Wireless*, Dolby was one of the first people to use the PPG 340/380 Wave Computer, an 8-voice polyphonic/polyrhythmic digital synthesizer and sequencer. This computer also has the ability to operate slide and film projections during Dolby's live performances. He's played with Lene Lovich and Bruce Woolley and the Camera Club. As a session musician he's recorded with the likes of Joan Armatrading, Foreigner, and the Fallout Club. His production credits include records by the Fallout Club, Low Noise, and Whodini.

Origin:	*British*
Label:	**Armageddon **Venice In Peril/ EMI †Jive*
Top L.P.:	***The Golden Age Of Wireless (1982).***
Pick Singles:	**Urges / Leipzig (1981), **Europa & The Pirate Twins / Therapy-Growth (1981), **Airwaves / The Wreck Of The Fairchild (1982),*** ***Radio Silence / "version" (1982),*** ***Windpower / Flying North (1982),*** *†Whodini — Magic's Wand / It's All In Mr. Magic's Wand (1982),* ***She Blinded Me With Science / One Of Our Submarines (1982).***

Duran Duran   p. 102

When they originally began recording in early '81, this five-piece Birmingham-based band were tagged "new romantic," while the critics tried to destroy their credibility in the music weeklies. Nowadays Duran is one of the hottest groups internationally. Their second album, *Rio*, stayed in the British top 30 for an entire year. Nick Rhodes has gone on to co-produce records for one of Britian's newest bands, Kajagoogoo.

Simon Le Bon, vocals; *Nick Rhodes,* keyboards, synthesizers; *Roger Taylor,* drums; *Andy Taylor,* guitar; *John Taylor,* bass.

Origin:	*British*
Label:	*Harvest/EMI*
Top L.P.'s:	*Duran Duran (1981), Rio (1982).*
Pick Singles:	*Planet Earth / Late Bar (1981), Girls On Film / Faster Than Light (1981), My Own Way / Like An Angel (1981), Hungry Like The Wolf / Careless Memories "Live" (1982), Save A Prayer / Hold Back The Rain (1982), Rio (Parts 1 & 2) / My Own Way (1982) Is There Something I Should Know / Faith In This Colour (1983).*

The English Beat   p. 58

Although the English Beat don't consider themselves a ska group, they first came to recognition during 1979, when they were signed to 2-Tone Records. Ska originally became popular in Britain during the early '60s. Like reggae, bluebeat, and calypso, ska originated from the island sounds of Jamaica and Barbados. Unlike reggae, ska is a rockier, uptempo music which usually features saxophone. The English Beat have changed severely since their early days when they were signed to the 2-Tone roster. Nowadays, their music seems to be divided into two categories: commercial pop and psychedelic dub.

Andy Cox, bass; *David Steele,* guitar; *Ranking Roger,* vocals, percussion; *Dave Wakeling,* vocals, guitar; *Everett Moreton,* drums, percussion; *Dave Blockhead,* keyboards; *Wesley Magoogan,* horns.

Origin:	*British*
Labels:	**2-Tone **Sire †I.R.S. ††Go-Feet*
Top L.P.'s:	***I Just Can't Stop It (1980),*** ***Wha'ppen? (1981), †Special Beat Service (1982).***
Pick Singles:	**Tears Of A Clown / Ranking Full Stop (1979), ††Hands Off...She's Mine / Twist & Crawl ('80),* *††Mirror In The Bathroom / Jackpot (1980), ††Hit It / Which Side Of The Bed...? (1981), ††Jeanette / March Of The Swivelheads (1982),* *††Save It For Later / What's Your Best Thing? ††Can't Get Used To Losing You (remix) / Spar Wid Me (1983).*

ESG p. 27

The Bronx. New York City's other side of the fence. Mrs. Scroggins wanted her daughters to do something creative instead of getting in trouble. She bought them instruments and inspired them to make their own kind of music. And that's exactly what her girls did. They formed a group called Emerald, Sapphire & Gold and hooked up with 99 Records' mainman Ed Bahlman. Within a year (1981) they released a startlingly "fresh" sounding 12" E.P. featuring the infectious single *You're No Good*.

The Scroggins Sisters — *Renee*, vocals, guitar; *Deborah*, bass, vocals; *Valerie*, drums, vocals; *Marie*, conga, vocals; and the newest addition, *Mr. Tito Libran*, conga.

Origin:	American
Labels:	*99 **Factory
Top L.P.:	*Debut L.P. coming soon.
Dance Faves:	*E S G 12" six-song E.P. featuring *You're No Good, Moody, UFO, Earn It,* and *Hey!* (1981), **You're No Good, UFO, Moody* (1981), *Dance To The Beat Of Moody,* 12" three-song E.P. (1982).

Eurythmics p. 42

The nucleus of Eurythmics (a term that describes a new method of teaching music), Annie Lennox and Dave Stewart, originally experienced success when their previous group, The Tourists, had a hit single in '79 with their rendition of *I Only Want To Be With You*. Eurythmics use synthesizers, and yet, Annie and Dave stress that they're not predominantly synthetic. They mix acoustic and electronic sounds — the synthes are used to enhance, to add whatever their image of a song should be. Upon recording their latest album, *Sweet Dreams*, the duo purchased their own recording equipment and ended up recording the L.P. on their own 8-track portable studio.

Annie Lennox, lead vocals; *Dave Stewart*, synthes, guitar, live mixing; *Mickey Gallagher*, keyboards, synthes; *Clem Burke*, drums; *Eddi Reader*, backing vocals, percussion.

Origin:	Scottish/British
Label:	RCA
Top L.P.'s:	*The Garden* (1981), *Sweet Dreams Are Made Of This* (1982).
Pick Singles:	*Never Gonna Cry Again / Le Sinistre* (1981), *Belinda / Heartbeat, Heartbeat* (1981), *This Is The House / Home Is Where The Heart Is* (1982), *The Walk/ Step On The Beast / The Walk Pt. II* (1982), *Love Is A Stranger / Monkey, Monkey* (1982), *Sweet Dreams Are Made of This / I Could Give You (A Mirror)* (1982).

Fad Gadget p. 12

Frank Tovey is the driving force behind Fad Gadget, possibly Mute Records' most intelligent, worthwhile signing to date. Frank originally studied performance art at college, where he acquired a passion for theatrics. Tovey is constantly changing his recording techniques and rarely works with the same musicians twice. These days he leaves the playing to his newly recruited musicians so that he can concentrate on his singing and the theatrical aspects of his outrageous performances.

Origin:	British
Label:	Mute
Top L.P.'s:	*Fireside Favorites* (1980), *Incontinent* (1981), *Under The Flag* (1982).
Pick Singles:	*Back To Nature / The Box* (1979), *Ricky's Hand / Handshake* (1980), *Fireside Favorite / Insecticide* (1980), *Make Room / Lady Shave* (1981), *Saturday Night Special / Swallow It Live* (1981), *King Of The Flies / Plain Clothes* (1982), *Life On The Line / 4M* (1982), *For Whom The Bells Toll / Love Parasite* (1982).

Falco p. 14

Originally a jazz student at the Vienna Music Conservatory, Falco played improvisational jazz with friends in his spare time. Falco joined what was to have been Austria's biggest rock band, Dradiwaberl, and played on their two L.P.'s *Psychoterror* and *McRonalds' Massacre*. But it wasn't until Falco won critical acclaim for *Ganz Wien* (All Vienna), a pop single that became something of a national anthem for Viennese youth, that things really started rolling. By the autumn of '81 Falco went solo and recorded the single *Der Kommissar* and the album *Einzelhaft* (Solitary Confinement). In 1982 *Der Kommissar* virtually made Falco an overnight success throughout Austria, Germany and Switzerland. Months later even North America started dancing to the funky German rap rhythms of *Kommissar*. By March of '83 it was the first time a single sung entirely in German went gold in Canada.

Origin:	Viennese
Labels:	*Gig **A&M
Top L.P.'s:	*Psychoterror* (1980), *McRonalds' Massacre* (1981), **Einzelhaft* (1982).
Pick Singles:	*Ganz Wien* (1980), **Der Kommissar,* 12" E.P. featuring *Auf Der Flucht* and *Helden Von Heute* (1982).

Fashion p. 84

Although Fashion originally formed in '78, they've undergone several unexpected personnel changes. In '78 they were a trio who played very punky reggae political songs. Founding members, keyboardist (then bassist) Mulligan and drummer Dik Daviss resurfaced with a new look and sound in '82. They landed a recording deal with Arista Records, and along with newcomers bassist Martin Recchi and guitarist/vocalist De Harriss, released a new album *Fabrique*. Unfortunately, lead vocalist De Harriss left Fashion during the latter half of '82. His replacement was Troy Tate formerly of the now defunct Teardrop Explodes, but only recently, he too left the group. The remaining members — Mulligan, Daviss and Recchi — are currently putting the finishing touches on the forthcoming album.

Mulligan, keyboards, synthes; *Martin Recchi*, bass; *Dik Daviss*, drums.

Origin:	*British*
Labels:	**Fashion Music / I.R.S.* ***Arista*
Top L.P.'s:	**Product Perfect* (1979), ***Fabrique* (1982).
Pick Singles:	**Steady Eddie Steady / Killing Time* (1978), **Citinite / Wastelife* (1979), **Silver Blades / A Deeper Cut* (1979), ***Move On / Mutant Dance Move* (1981), ***Streetplayer-Mechanik / Mutant Mix Mechanik* (1982), ***Something In Your Picture / Alternative Playback* (1982), ***Love Shadow / Let's Play Dirty* (1982).

The Fixx   p. 74

Like A Flock Of Seagulls, the Fixx, for some unexplained reason, broke the North American market before they were accepted on their own British turf. During 1982 Canadians and Americans swooned to the dramatic intensity of the single *Stand Or Fall*. Former Teardrop Explodes' bassist, Alfie Aguis, although not featured on the group's debut, eventually joined the Fixx crew on their North American tour during '82. The Fixx have just released their follow-up album *Reach The Beach* and accompanying single *Saved By Zero*.

Cy Curnin, vocals; *Jamie West-Oram*, guitar; *Adam Woods*, drums; *Rupert Greenall*, keyboards, synthes; *Alfie Aguis*, bass.

Origin:	*British*
Labels:	**Polydor* ***MCA*
Top L.P.'s:	***Shuttered Room* (1982), ***Reach The Beach* (1983).
Pick Singles:	**Lost Planes / I've Been There Before* (1981), ***Stand Or Fall / The Strain* (1982), ***Red Skies / Sinking Island* (1982), ***Saved By Zero / Overboard* (1983).

A Flock of Seagulls   p. 127

Originally from Liverpool, vocalist/keyboardist Mike Score adopted "A Flock Of Seagulls," which, in fact, first appeared as a lyric in the Stranglers' song *Toiler Of The Sea*, and formed the Gulls in the winter of 1979. From there they recorded two singles with former Be Bop Deluxe guitarist Bill Nelson — *Talking* and *Telecommunication* — the latter being a huge success. It was their self-titled debut album and single *I Ran* that virtually made them a household name throughout North America in '82. Come '83 their second album *Listen* and accompanying singles, *Wishing* and *Nightmares*, were released and, interestingly enough, a re-mixed version of their first single *Talking* was included on the L.P. as well.

Mike Score, lead vocals, keyboards, guitar; *Paul Reynolds*, lead guitar, vocals; *Frank Maudsley*, bass, vocals; *Ali Score*, drums.

Origin:	*British*
Labels:	**Cocteau* ***Jive*
Top L.P.'s:	***A Flock Of Seagulls* (1982), ***Listen* (1983).
Pick Singles:	**Talking / Factory Music* (1981), ***Telecommunication / Intro* (1981), ***Modern Love Is Automatic / DNA* (1981), ***I Ran / Pick Me Up* (1982), ***Space Age Love Song / Windows* (1982), ***Wishing (if I had a Photograph of You) / Committed* (1982), ***Nightmares / Rosenmontang* (1983).

John Foxx   p. 73

Foxx is a multi-instrumentalist and producer who originally founded Ultravox in 1977. By '79 Foxx left Ultravox to pursue a solo career. He went on to record two albums, *Metamatic* and *The Garden*, on his own Metal Beat label. Foxx was one of the first people in Britain to combine electronics and rock and topped it all off by penning mysterious, surreal lyrics. At the moment Foxx is working on several projects, including his first novel *The Quiet Man*, and his forthcoming third solo album produced by Mike Howlett and Zeus B. Held.

Origin:	*British*
Labels:	**Gull* ***Island* †*Metal Beat / Virgin*
Top L.P.'s:	***Ultravox!* (1977), ***Ha Ha Ha* (1977), ***Systems Of Romance* (1978), †*Metamatic* (1980), †*The Garden* (1981), †*The Golden Section* (1983).
Pick Singles:	**Ain't Misbehavin' / Monkey Jive* (alias "Dennis Leigh" of Tiger Lilly) (1976), ***Dangerous Rhythm / My Sex* (1977), ***Quiet Men / Cross Fade* (1978), †*Underpass / Film One* (1980), †*Burning Car / 20th Century* (1980), †*Europe After The Rain / This Jungle* (1981), †*Endlessly / Young Man* (1982), †*Endlessly* (re-release) (1983).

Johnny Dee Fury   p. 19

The resurgence of rockabilly? I don't think it ever went away. Rockabilly was deliberately ignored when rock'n'roll got the big push in the late '50s. Canada's Johnny Dee Fury opts for an extremely poppy approach which still retains the spirit of early rock'n'roll. Dee Fury, a guitarist/vocalist and piano man, like a lot of today's new rockabilly artists, is re-introducing rock'n'roll to anyone and everyone who is concerned. He's playing rock with the roll left in it. And that's what's missing from so many of today's new groups — the "roll."

Origin:	*Canadian*
Label:	*Orient/RCA*
Top L.P.:	*Born To Bop* (1982).
Pick Singles:	*Can't Stop The Bop / Wildcat* (1982), *This Heart's On Fire / Coyote* (1982), *Knock Knock / Come Back Baby* (1982), *Coyote / Rockabilly Rooster* (1983).

Peter Gabriel p. 28

During July of '82, prior to the release of his fourth solo album, Peter Gabriel organized WOMAD, a three day multinational arts festival in Bath, England. When Gabriel performed his music he was accompanied by the Bristol Afro-Caribbean dance rhythm group Ekome and an Indian violinist called Shankar. The interesting thing about Peter Gabriel is the fact that he's always willing to try out new ideas. In the mid '70s he left the superstar league of Genesis and has since spread his creativity over a wide range of projects.

Origin: British
Labels: *Charisma **Charisma / Geffen
Top L.P.'s: *Peter Gabriel I (1977), *Peter Gabriel II (1978), *Peter Gabriel III (1980), **Peter Gabriel IV (Security) (1982), **Plays Live (1983).
Pick Singles: *D.I.Y. / Perspective (1978), *Games Without Frontiers / The Start / I Don't Remember (1980), *No Self Control / Lead A Normal Life (1980), *Biko / Shosholoza / Jetzt Kommit Die Flut (1980), **Shock The Monkey / Soft Dog (1982), *I Have The Touch / Across The River (1982).

Grandmaster Flash p. 44

Grandmaster Flash & The Furious Five — one deejay, one assistant and five emcees from the heart of the Bronx — took the funky appeal of Rick James and Sly Stone and developed their own energetic, slick street show, one that grooved and moved their dance crazy audiences. Flash (Joseph Saddler) was one of the first deejays who cultivated various ways of re-arranging the actual sound of a record. With several records at his fingertips, both 7- and 12-inch, Flash would mix them to the beat of a syncopated rhythm track, sometimes treating certain records with echo effects and other devices. With the stylus firmly planted in the vinyl groove, audiences would marvel as he distorted the inherent sound by scratching, backspinning or phasing.

Grandmaster Flash, deejay; *Melle Mel*, emcee; *Kid Creole*, emcee; *Cowboy*, emcee; *Mr. Ness*, emcee; *Rahiem*, emcee; *E-Z Mike*, assistant.

Origin: American
Label: Sugarhill
Top L.P.: Grandmaster Flash & The Furious Five (1982).
12" Dance Mixes: Freedom / Instrumental (1980), The Adventures Of Grandmaster Flash On The Wheels Of Steel / Party Mix (1981), It's Nasty (Genius Of Love) / Scorpio (1981), Birthday Party / Instrumental (1981), Showdown (The Furious Five Meet The Sugarhill Gang) / Instrumental (1981), The Message / Instrumental (1982), Message II (Survival) / Instrumental (1983), New York, New York / Instrumental (1983).

Robert Fripp p. 21

In the '60s and early '70s this influential guitarist captivated audiences with his first "progressive" group, King Crimson. Now he's continuing his Drive to 1984, playing Frippertronics and giving lectures whenever possible. Interestingly enough, Fripp reformed Crimson in 1981 with original drummer Bill Bruford. Since 1979 Robert's been unbelievably prolific. He released the controversial *Exposure* solo album and began writing a series of articles related to the politics and economics of the music industry for *Musician, Player and Listener* and *Sound International*. His production credits include Daryl Hall, The Roaches, and Peter Gabriel. His guitar playing has graced albums by Blondie, Gabriel, and Bowie, and most recently he collaborated with Andy Summers of the Police. You may even remember him when he formed The League Of Gentlemen in 1981 with Barry Andrews, Sarah Lee and Johnny Toobad.

Origin: British
Labels: *E.G. **Polydor †A&M
Recent L.P.'s: **No Pussyfooting (1974), **Evening Star (1975), *Exposure (1979), *God Save The Queen / Under Heavy Manners (1980), *The League Of Gentlemen (1981), *Let The Power Fall (1981), *Discipline (1981), *Beat (1982), †I Advance Masked (1982).

Gun Club p. 130

The Gun Club seem to be the only group experimenting with traditional American blues. Vocalist/frontman Pierce admits the Club doesn't play blues the same way most blues virtuosos do. Although they adhere to a similar technique, they are reinterpretating blues, distorting it, tearing it apart and putting it back together in their own way.

Jim Duckworth, guitar; *Dee Pop*, drums; *Patricia Morrison*, bass; *Jeffery Lee Pierce*, vocals, guitar, piano.

Origin: American
Labels: *Ruby/Slash **Beggars Banquet †Animal
Top L.P.'s: *Fire Of Love (1981), †Miami (1982).
Pick Singles: **Sex Beat / Ghost On The Highway (1981), †Fire Of Love / Walking With The Beast (1982), †Death Party, 12" E.P. featuring The House on Highland Ave., The Lie, The Light of the World and Come Back Jim (1983).

Nina Hagen p. 45

East Berlin's 29-year-old reigning queen of pop psychedelia, Nina Hagen, could very well be the only female performer with twenty different personalities rolled into one. Her vocal ability is quite unorthodox. Inevitably, she was signed to CBS in West Germany and a debut L.P. ensued in '78. Now, after three albums and several singles, Nina is presently residing in Los Angeles with her baby daughter Cosma Shiva, making preparations for her next album.

Origin: German
Labels: *CBS **Ariola

Top L.P.'s:	*Nina Hagen Band (1978), **Cha Cha The Soundtrack from the Film (1979), *Unbehagen (1979) *Nunsexmonkrock (1982).
Pick Singles:	*Unbeschreiblich Weiblich / Der Spinner (1979), *T.V. Glotzer / Naturtrane (1979), *African Reggae / Wau Wau (1980), *My Way / Alptraum / No Way, 12" (1980), *Smack Jack / Cosma Shiva (1982).

Heaven 17　　　　　　　　　　　p. 17

When Ian Craig Marsh and Martyn Ware left the Human League at the beginning of 1981, they were in huge debt to Virgin Records. Suddenly they wanted to cut down on expenses. They formed B.E.F. (British Electric Foundation), their very own production company which not only facilitates their group Heaven 17, but has since produced work for Hot Gossip and the *Music Of Quality And Distinction* project which featured such renowned vocalists as Tina Turner, Gary Glitter, and Sandie Shaw. This time around Heaven 17 confess they spent a lot more time in the studio developing ideas on their recent *Luxury Gap* L.P. as opposed to *Penthouse*. Looking back on the *Penthouse* L.P., Heaven 17 all agree that half of it had a naive charm but it was "definitely underdeveloped." Even though *Luxury Gap* was recorded in a 48 track studio, the album isn't strictly synthetic — an orchestra was used extensively and the overall feel echoes the big band era, jazz, swing, funk, soul and contemporary pop.

  Glenn Gregory, lead vocals; *Martyn Ware*, synthes, keyboards, electronic percussion, programming; *Ian Craig Marsh*, electronic bass programming, synthes, keyboards.

Origin:	*British*
Label:	*B.E.F. / Virgin*
Top L.P.'s:	*Music For Stowaways* (on cassette only, 1981), *Music For Listening To* (1981), *Penthouse & Pavement* (1981), *Music of Quality And Distinction* (1982), *The Luxury Gap* (1983).
Pick Singles:	*(We Don't Need This) Fascist Groove Thang / The Decline Of The West* (1981), *I'm Your Money / Are Everything* (1981), *Play To Win / Play* (1981), *Anyone Who Had A Heart / Instrumental* (1982), *Ball Of Confusion / Instrumental* (1982), *Let Me Go / Instrumental* (1982), *Temptation / We Live So Fast* (1983).

Richard Hell　　　　　　　　　　p. 95

In the mid '70s Hell was solely responsible for inventing the look, smell and taste of punk rock. Richard's previous groups included the Neon Boys and Television, both of which featured Tom Verlaine. Due to musical differences Hell left the original line-up of Television to play bass guitar for the Heartbreakers. Finally, in 1976 Hell formed his own group, Richard Hell and the Voidoids, with Ivan Julian on rhythm guitar, Marc (Ramones) Bell on drums and the incomparable Robert Quine on lead guitar. In 1977 Hell's debut album *Blank Generation* not only was the most powerful punk record of the '70s but it also paved the way for a million imitators and was responsible for triggering the punk revolution in Britain in '77.

Origin:	*American*
Labels:	*Sire **Red Star †Radar ††Shake ‡Ork*
Top L.P.'s:	*Blank Generation (1977), **Destiny Street (1982).*
Pick Singles:	*Blank Generation / Love Comes In Spurts (1977), ‡I Could Live With You In Another World / Blank Generation / You Gotta Lose (1977), †The Kid With The Replaceable Head / I'm Your Man (1978), ††The Neon Boys E.P. featuring That's All I Know (Right Now) and the original version of Love Comes In Spurts plus two Voidoids tracks — Time and Don't Die (1980).*

Billy Idol　　　　　　　　　　　p. 39

Billy Idol, former vocalist for the now defunct British punk band Generation X, is currently pursuing a solo career in New York City. Along with the likes of the Clash and the Pistols, Gen X were one of the first punk/pop crossover bands to pen several hit singles. At the beginning of their brief, scattered career, Gen X recorded such classics as *Your Generation* and *Wild Youth*. In 1980 Gen X recorded what was to have been their final single, a surprising dance floor hit *Dancing With Myself*. One year later Idol landed a solo contract with Chrysalis Records, and released a re-mixed version of *Dancing* coupled with a rendition of Tommy James' *Mony Mony* on his debut E.P. *Don't Stop*. Come '82, Idol released his debut self-titled solo album.

Origin:	*British*
Label:	*Chrysalis*
Top L.P.'s:	*Generation X (1978), Valley Of The Dolls (1979), Kiss Me Deadly (1981), Billy Idol (1982).*
Pick Singles:	*Your Generation / Day By Day (1977), Ready, Steady, Go / No No No (1978), King Rocker / Gimmie Some Truth (1979), Dancing With Myself / Ugly Rash (1980), Hot In The City / Dead On Arrival (1982), White Wedding / Hole In The Wall (1982).*

Rick James　　　　　　　　　　p. 114

James, a native of Buffalo, New York, moved to Toronto in the late '60s where he played music on the Yorkville/Yonge Street club circuit for nine years, right up until the mid '70s. James gained international recognition with the release of his fifth album *Street Songs* ('81). From it, the singles *Give It To Me Baby* and *Super Freak* made Rick James' hot'n'steamy sexual funk a satisfying dance favorite.

Origin:	*American*
Label:	*Motown*
Top L.P.'s:	*Come And Get It (1978), Bustin' Out (1979), Fire It Up (1979), Garden Of Love (1980), Street Songs (1981), Throwin' Down (1982).*
Pick Singles:	*Big Time / Island Lady (1978), Bustin' Out / Sexy Lady (1979), Ghetto Life / Below The Funk (1981), Mary Jane / Dream Maker (1979), Give It To Me Baby / Don't Give Up On Love (1981), Super Freak / Super Freak Pt. Two (1981), Hard To Get / Instrumental (1982), Dance Wit' Me / Dance Wit' Me Pt. Two (1982).*

Japan   p. 60

When punk was the main rave in the U.K. during 1978, Japan were heavily criticized by the British music press for being New York Doll post-glam rip-off artists. They wore make-up, had bleached and coloured hair, and their clothes were chic, trashy, and very androgenous. Musically, they were compared to Roxy Music, especially David Sylvian's vocal intonation. At first Japan were superstars in the Orient. Even Toronto, Canada became infatuated with the group's first two albums *Adolescent Sex* and *Obscure Alternatives*. It is ironic, however, that the group recently split just when they were beginning to get successful in their native England.

Richard Barbieri, keyboards, synthes; *Mick Karn*, bass, sax, oboe; *Steve Jansen*, drums, electronic and keyboard percussion; *Masami Tsuchiya*, guitar; *David Sylvian*, vocals, keyboards, tapes, guitar.

Origin:	*British*
Labels:	**Ariola-Hansa **Virgin*
Top L.P.'s:	**Adolescent Sex (1978), *Obscure Alternatives (1978), *Quiet Life (1979), **Gentlemen Take Polaroids (1980), **The Tin Drum (1981), **Oil On Canvas (1983).*
Pick Singles:	**Don't Rain On My Parade / Stateline (1978), *Quiet Life / Hallowe'en (1979), *Second That Emotion / Quiet Life (1980), **Art Of Parties / Life Without Buildings (1981), **Ghosts / Art Of Parties (version) (1981), **Mick Karn's Sensitive / The Sound Of Waves (1982), **David Sylvian & Riuichi Sakamoto's Bamboo Music / Bamboo Houses (1982), **Nightporter (remix) / Ain't That Peculiar (1982), *Life In Tokyo (remix) / Tokyo (Theme) (1982), **Canton "Live" / Visions of China "Live" (1983).*

Joan Jett   p. 96

At 16, Joan Jett was discovered by L.A.'s Kim Fowley. She played rhythm guitar and sang vocals for the Runaways, Sunset Boulevard's first teen dream female pop group. Their 1976 debut album featured their first massive hit single, *Cherry Bomb,* and an appealing rendition of the Lou Reed classic, *Rock And Roll.* After several personnel changes, the Runaways eventually disbanded in late '78. Joan went to England to record a rendition of *You Don't Own Me* produced by Steve Jones and Paul Cook, formerly of the Sex Pistols. The "b" side featured an early version of what was to become her million-selling hit, *I Love Rock'n'Roll.* Now Joan fronts her very own band, the Blackhearts.

Ricky Byrd, guitar, vocals; *Lee Crystal*, drums; *Gary Ryan*, bass, vocals; *Joan Jett*, lead vocals, rhythm guitar.

Origin:	*American*
Labels:	**Mercury **Cherry Red †Ariola ††Boardwalk*
Top L.P.'s:	**Runaways (1976), *Queens Of Noise (1977), *Live In Japan (1977), *Waitin' For The Night (1977), *And Now...The Runaways (1978), **Flaming Schoolgirls (1980), †Joan Jett (1980), — This L.P. was re-released a year later under the title Bad Reputation., ††I Love Rock'n'Roll (1981).*
Pick Singles:	**Cherry Bomb / Blackmail (1976), *Midnight Music / Neon Angels On The Road To Ruin (1977), *School Days / Wasted (1977), You Don't Own Me / I Love Rock'n'Roll (1979 — Vertigo Records), †Jezebel / Bad Reputation (1980), ††I Love Rock'n'Roll / Love Is Pain (1982), ††Crimson & Clover / Oh Woe Is Me (1982), ††You Don't Know What You've Got / (I'm Gonna) Run Away "live" (1982).*

KaS Product   p. 66

KaS Product mixes crude, harsh electronic rhythms with soulful, jazz-like vocals. Unlike the British-based synthe duo Yazoo, KaS Product literally put the screws to their electronics and purposely try to make the sound frenzied and energetic. Vocalist/guitarist Mona Soyoc originally had a strong passion for jazz and blues, while synthesist Spatsz used to play with several hardcore punk bands in his native Nancy, France.

Mona Soyoc, vocals, guitar; *Spatsz*, synthes, keyboards, electronic percussion.

Origin:	*French*
Labels:	**Punk **RCA †Light/RCA*
Top L.P.'s:	***Try Out (1981), †By Pass (1983).*
Pick Singles:	**Mind, 7" E.P. featuring Seven, Black & Noir and Dr. Insane (1980), *Take Me Tonight / In Need / Malena (1980), **Pussy X / Never Come Back (1981), †Chinatown / Loony Bin (1983).*

Killing Joke   p. 118

Their music is aggressive, deafening and explosive. Killing Joke are the recurring nightmare that reminds us of our human mistakes and short term solutions. If you're looking for love songs, forget it. Their music is intuitive and so are their audiences. In fact, the British-based Jokesters have often said that their music is intuition taken to its extreme. Their tribal, discordant, metallic wall of sound us as creative as it is destructive.

Jaz Coleman, vocals, keyboards; *Paul Ferguson*, drums; *Geordie*, guitar; *Dave Raven*, bass.

Origin:	*British*
Labels:	**Malicious Damage / EG* ***Malicious Damage*
Top L.P.'s:	**Killing Joke* (1980), **What's This FOR!* (1981), **Revelations* (1982), ***"HA"*, 10" live E.P. recorded at Larry's Hideaway in Toronto (1982).
Pick Singles:	***Are You Receiving / Turn To Red / Nervous System* (1979), ***Psyche / War Dance* (1980), **Requiem / Change* (1981), **Follow The Leaders / Tension* (1981), **Empire Song / Brilliant* (1982), **Chop-Chop / Good Samaritan* (1982), **Birds Of A Feather / Sun Goes Down / Flock The B Side* (1982).

Leisure Process p. 136

Leisure Process International are what you'd refer to as "an unlikely pair of adventurous opportunists." Glasgow-bred lyricist/vocalist Ross Middleton was the founding member of Positive Noise, a magical little monster group that mixed uptempo percussion and guitar textures in the similar vein of Joy Division's true blue gloom. Positive Noise's two cult singles, *Give Me Passion* and *Charm*, not only turned a lot of heads but they influenced any contemporary pop group you care to mention, from New Order to ABC. Saxophonist/composer Gary Barnacle makes up the second half of L.P.I. He could quite conceivably be the busiest session sax player going at the moment. His past credits include Level 42, the Clash, Bush Tetras, Soft Cell, Visage, Teardrop Explodes, Nona Hendryx and the Stray Cats to name a few.

Ross Middleton, guitar, bass, keyboards, lead vocals; *Gary Barnacle*, saxophone, keyboards, flute, Linn drums.

Origin:	*British*
Label:	*Epic*
Top L.P.:	*Debut L.P. not yet released.*
Pick Singles:	*Love Cascade / The Fluke* (1982), *A Way You'll Never Be / Rachel Dreams* (1982), *Cashflow / The Emigre* (1983), Anxiety / Company B (1983).

The Lords of the New Church p. 64

Stiv Bator, one-time vocalist for Cleveland, Ohio's punk group the Dead Boys, has finally landed himself in the timely position of spokesman for the Lords Of The New Church. Bator, along with guitarist Brian James (ex-Damned), bassist Dave Tregunna (ex-Sham 69) and drummer Nicky Turner (ex-Barracuda) have more or less been bridesmaids to success. The fact is, they've never really had it. This time around Bator sings about how the riches of organized religion could be used as a political tool to start a possible holy war. Bator insists America's very dangerous right now ever since the state started working side by side with the church.

Stiv Bator, vocals, attitude; *Dave Tregunna*, bass; *Brian James*, guitar; *Nicky Turner*, drums.

Origin:	*American/British*
Labels:	**Illegal **I.R.S.*
Top L.P.:	***The Lords Of The New Church* (1982).
Pick Singles:	**New Church / Livin' On Livin'* (1982), **Open Your Eyes / Girls Girls Girls* (1982), ***Russian Roulette / Young Don't Cry* (1982), ***Live For Today* (the Lords' rendition of the Grassroots' 1965 hit, this time produced by Todd Rundgren) (1983).

Lounge Lizards p. 97

Brothers John and Evan Lurie, the nucleus of the New York-based Lounge Lizards, were originally raised in Massachusetts. They formed the group in 1979 and recorded one album for E.G. Records. Today they are signed to the independent Europa label and have just released their long awaited second album, this time a live effort, entitled *Live At The Drunken Boat*. The Lizards are taking the spirit of traditional jazz, revitalizing it, and playing it to an entirely new audience in a new music environment. In 1981 the Lizards' self-titled debut album was produced by Ted Macero, the same producer who recorded Miles Davis, Charles Mingus and Thelonious Monk. Original compositions aside, the debut also featured some memorable renditions including Earl Hagen's *Harlem Nocturne* and Thelonius Monk's *Epistrophy* and *Well You Needn't*.

Tony Garnier, acoustic bass; *Dougie Bowne*, drums; *Peter Zummo*, trombone; *Evan Lurie*, acoustic piano; *John Lurie*, alto sax.

Origin:	*American*
Labels:	**E.G. **Europa*
Top L.P.'s:	**The Lounge Lizards* (1981), ***Live At The Drunken Boat* (1983).
Cassette:	*Stomping At The Corona "live", New Musical Express Dancin' Master* (1981).

Lene Lovich p. 86

Mariene Premilovich. To her admirers, she's better known as Lene Lovich, a slavic Detroit-bred singer/songwriter who is currently based in England. The woman with the melodic yodel and high-pitched squeal has been entertaining audiences since the release of her 1979 debut L.P., *Stateless*, and the single, *Lucky Number*. A second L.P., *Flex*, was recorded in 1980, and to coincide with its release, Lene embarked on a sell-out tour of Europe and North America. A year later everybody in the clubs were dancing to *New Toy*, co-written by Lene and British synthesist Thomas Dolby. She re-emerged in '82 playing sax on Tom Verlaine's *Words From The Front* L.P. In August of the same year, Lene began rehearsals for a stage musical based on the life story of Mata Hari which she co-wrote with guitarist/partner Les Chappell. She recently graced the airwaves with her third album

No-Man's-Land and the triumphant single, *It's You, Only You (Mein Schmerz)*.

Origin:	American
Label:	Stiff
Top L.P.:	*Stateless* (1979), *Flex* (1980), *No-Man's-Land* (1982).
Pick Singles:	*Lucky Number / Home* (1978), *Say When / One Lonely Heart* (1979), *Birdsong / Trixi* (1979), *Angels / The Fly* (1980), *What Will I Do Without You / Joan* (1980), *New Toy / Cats Away* (1981), *It's You, Only You (Mein Schmerz) / Blue* (1982).

Madonna   p. 34

Madonna, a native of Detroit, is a rare exception when it comes to music and dance. As a child, she learned ballet and eventually moved to New York where she studied modern dance with the likes of the great Pearl Lang and Twyla Tharp. She purposely sings and dances to a pre-recorded tape instead of using a live band. Each song coincides with a dance routine tastefully choreographed by Madonna and her fellow background dancers.

Origin:	American
Label:	Sire
Top L.P.:	*Lucky Star* (1983).
Pick Singles:	*Everybody / Dub version* (1982), *Burning Up / Physical Attraction* (1983).

Martha and the Muffins   p. 40

In 1980, a relatively unknown Canadian pop group, Martha and the Muffins, scored a Top Ten single *(Echo Beach)* in the British pop charts. Since then the group have been recording albums on a regular basis picking up various awards in the Canadian music industry. Martha and the Muffins believe in individuals working together to create an atmosphere of sound. And that's what they've been doing on their third and fourth albums, especially their latest, *Danseparc*. Their current sound isn't indicative of their hit singles of yesteryear; they've matured considerably.

Jocelyne Lanois, bass, vocals; *Nick Kent*, drums, percussion; *Martha Johnson*, lead vocals, keyboards, guitar; *Mark Gane*, vocals, guitar, keyboards.

Origin:	Canadian
Labels:	*Muffin Music **Dindisc †Current/RCA
Top L.P.'s:	**Metro Music (1980), **Trance & Dance (1980), **This Is The Ice Age (1981), †Danseparc (1983).
Pick Singles:	*Insect Love / Suburban Dream (1979), **Echo Beach / Teddy The Dink (1980), **About Insomnia / 146 (1980), **Women Around The World At Work / 22 In Cincinnati (1981), **Swimming / Little Sounds (1981), †Danseparc, 12" mix featuring These Dangerous Machines (1983), †World Without Borders / Boys in the Bushes (1983).

Men Without Hats   p. 126

This group from Montreal started recording electronic-based music during 1980. They released their own *Folk Of The '80s* E.P. (which was subsequently re-released by Stiff America a year later). Now they've become successful electro-acoustic pop stars in Canada due to the 1982 release of their debut L.P., *Rhythm Of Youth*.

Ivan, lead vocals, electronics, guitar, piano, percussion; *Allan McCarthy*, electronics, piano, percussion; *Stefan Doroschuk*, guitar, violin; *Colin Doroschuk*, guitar, guitar synthesizer.

Origin:	Canadian
Labels:	*Stiff America **Statik/Sire †Backstreet
Top L.P.:	†**Rhythm Of Youth (1982).
Pick Singles:	*Folk Of The '80s, 12" E.P. featuring Modern(e) Dancing, Utter Space and more (1980), **Antartica / Modern Dancing (1982), **I Got The Message / Utter Space (1982), †**The Safety Dance, 12" E.P. featuring I Got The Message and Antartica (1983).

Minny Pops   p. 104

This prominent Dutch group embarked on their first North American tour in 1981. The name "Minny Pops" is derived from one of the original rhythm machines on the market, the "Kong Mini-Pop." The original line-up featured guitar, bass, rhythm machine and vocals. Vocalist/lyricist Wally Van Middendorp admits Minny Pops concentrated on a singular style — "Early mechanical machine-like music." Since their inception, Minny Pops are still projecting their unusual blend of distorted textures and electronic rhythms.

P. Mulder, bass, synthe; *O. Roovers*, drums, percussion; *W. Dekker*, synthesizers; *W. Middendorp*, lead vocals, synthe.

Origin:	Dutch
Labels:	*Plurex **Factory †Factory-Benelux
Top L.P.'s:	*Drastic Measures, Drastic Movement (1979), †Sparks In A Dark Room (1982).
Pick Singles:	*Kojak / Footsteps / Nervous (1979), *Minny Pops "Live" featuring Mental, Night Out and Dolphins Spurt (1980), **Dolphins Spurt / Goddess (1980), †Love In My Heart / Een Kus (flexi-disc from Dutch magazine Vinyl 1981), †Time / Lights (1982), **Secret Story / Island (1982).

Modern English   p. 120

If inspiration and spontaneity are the two ingredients that make pop a necessity, not a luxury, then groups like Modern English just might change our preconceptions about the current state of new music. Modern English have been recording since 1979 with the *Silent World / Drowning Man* single on Limp Records. Their sound has matured and grown considerably over the past few years.

Robbie Grey, vocals; *Gary McDowell*, guitar; *Stephan*

Walker, synthesizers, keyboards; *Michael Conroy*, bass, *Richard Brown*, drums, percussion.

Origin:	*British*
Label:	*4.A.D.*
Top L.P.'s:	*Mesh And Lace* (1981), *After The Snow* (1982).
Pick Singles:	*Swans On Glass / Incident* (1980), *Gathering Dust / Tranquillity* (1980), *Smiles And Laughter / Mesh And Lace* (1981), *Life In The Gladhouse / Choicest View*, 12" (1982), *I Melt With You / The Prize* (1982).

Motorhead   p. 50

Motorhead is probably the only heavy metal band worth taking note of. They have their own unique following. Motorhead's fans admire their uncanny sense of humor and ability to deafen the hearing of the heaviest of headbangers. The name was originally derived from one of Hawkwind's song titles, the latter being bassist/vocalist Lemmy Kilmister's previous group. Original lead guitarist Eddie Clarke left the band in 1982 when Lemmy and drummer "Animal" recorded the country classic *Stand By Your Man* in Toronto with Wendy O. Williams singing lead vocals.

Lemmy Kilmister, lead vocals, bass; *Philthy Animal Taylor*, drums, percussion; *Brian Robertson*, guitar.

Origin:	*British*
Labels:	**Chiswick **Bronze †Liberty / United Artists*
Top L.P.'s:	**Motorhead* (1977), ***Bomber* (1979), *†On Parole* (1979), ***Overkill* (1979), ***Ace Of Spades* (1980), ***No Sleep Til' Hammersmith* "live" (1981), ***Iron Fist* (1982), ***Another Perfect Day* (1983).
Pick Singles:	***Overkill / Too Late, Too Late* (1979), ***No Class / Like A Nightmare* (1979), ***Bomber / Over The Top* (1979), ***Ace Of Spades / Dirty Love* (Christmas 12" 1980), ***Motorhead Live*, 12" E.P. featuring *Leaving Here, Stone Dead Forever, Dead Men Tell No Tales* and *Too Late, Too Late* (1980), ***Motorhead / Over The Top* "live" (1981), ***Iron Fist / Remember Me, I'm Gone* (1982). ***I Got Mine / Turn Your Head Around* (1983).

Nash the Slash   p. 125

The classically trained electric violinist first appeared in the early '70s with two Canadian progressive rock bands — Breathless and F.M. He formed his independent label, Cut-Throat Records, in '78. In February of 1980 he toured America with Gary Numan, and, in 1981, Nash supported Iggy Pop on his *Zombie Birdhouse* tour of America. Nash is currently finishing his latest E.P. — renditions of some of his favorite cover songs.

Origin:	*Canadian*
Labels:	**Cut-Throat **Dindisc †PVC*
Top L.P.'s:	**Bedside Companion*, 12" 4-track E.P. (1978), **Dreams & Nightmares* (1979), ***Children Of The Night* (1981), **Decomposing*, 12" 4-track E.P. (1981), **And You Thought You Were Normal* (1982).
Pick Singles:	**Dead Man's Curve / Swing Shift Soixante-Neuf* (1980), ***Dead Man's Curve / Reactor No. 2* (1981), ***19th Nervous Breakdown / Danger Zone*, (1981), ***Novel Romance / In A Glass Eye* (1981), *†Dance After Curfew / Womble / The Calling*, 12" E.P. (1983).

Bill Nelson   p. 116

Bill Nelson, former guitarist/songwriter for Be Bop Deluxe and Red Noise, is currently recording his own solo albums, soundtracks and producing and playing with other artists as well. In 1980 Nelson formed his own independent *Cocteau* label. He's produced records for the now defunct Skids, Nash the Slash, A Flock Of Seagulls, Gary Numan. He recently returned from Japan where he played on the Yellow Magic Orchestra's forthcoming album. During March of '83 Nelson toured England under the banner *Bill Nelson's Invisibility Exhibition* with the Yorkshire Actor's Theatre Company.

Origin:	*British*
Labels:	**Smile **Harvest †Cocteau ††Mercury/Phonogram*
Top L.P.'s:	**Northern Dream* (1971), ***Axe Victim* (1974), ***Futurama* (1975), ***Modern Music* (1976), ***Live In The Air Age* (1977), ***Drastic Plastic* (1978), ***Sound On Sound* (1979), *††Quit Dreaming And Get On The Beam* (1981), *†Das Kabinet* (1981), *††The Love That Whirls* (1982), *††Chimera*, 6-track E.P. (1983).
Pick Singles:	***Maid In Heaven / Sister Seagull* (1975), ***Kiss Of Light / Shine* (1976), ***Panic In The World / Blue As A Jewel* (1978), ***Furniture Music / Wonder Toys That Last Forever / Acquitted By Mirrors* (1979), *†Do You Dream In Colour?*, E.P. (1980), *††Banal / Mr. Magnetism Himself* (1981), *††Flaming Desire / The Passion* (1982).

Nico   p. 63

Originally an actress in Germany, Nico became an international celebrity when she joined the Velvet Underground in 1967. Her solo work produced such classics as *Marble Index, Chelsea Girl, Desert Shore,* and *The End*. Her recent work, including an album entitled *Drama Of Exile,* and an E.P. produced by Martin Hannett, has been unfortunately overlooked by trend-crazy journalists.

Origin:	German
Labels:	*MGM **Reprise †Island ††Aura ‡Flicknife ‡‡ 1/2 Records §Immediate
Top L.P.'s	*The Velvet Underground & Nico (1967), *Marble Index (1968), *Chelsea Girl (1971), **Desert Shore (1971), †The End (1974), *June 1, 1974 (1974), ††Drama Of Exile (1981).
Pick Singles:	§I'm Not Sayin'/Last Mile (1965), ‡Saeta / Vegas (1981), ‡‡Procession / All Tomorrow's Parties (1982).

Klaus Nomi   p. 18

Nomi was officially born in Bavaria, and after being classically trained as an opera singer, he eventually moved to New York City in the early '70s. By combining classical music and rock, he discovered that he could work within an entirely new aural framework. North America was introduced to Nomi's magical blend of opera, pop, and theatrics when he danced behind David Bowie on "Saturday Night Live" broadcast on American TV a few years ago. His second album, *Simple Man*, originally released in Europe in 1982, was only just released in North America a few months ago. His records have gone gold in Europe.

Origin:	German
Labels:	*RCA **A&M
Top L.P.'s:	*Klaus Nomi (1981), **Total Eclipse "live" on URGH! A Music War (1981), *Simple Man (1982).
Pick Singles:	*Nomi Song / The Cold Song (1981), *You Don't Own Me / Falling In Love Again (1981), *Lightning Strikes / Falling In Love Again (1982), *Ding Dong / ICUROK (1982), *Simple Man / Rubber Band Laser (1982).

Orchestral Manoeuvres in the Dark   p. 121

The inspiration for Liverpool-based OMD comes from the heart and soul. In 1982, after recording and performing their third album, *Architecture & Morality*, McCluskey and Humphreys financed their own exclusive label, *Telegraph Records*. OMD took a gamble with *Dazzle Ships*, and experimented with a lot of sound effects and unpredictable arrangements. The sound is contemporary, but with all their processed electronics and treatments OMD will never abandon the element of human compassion.

Paul Humphreys, keyboards, synthes, vocals; *Andy McCluskey*, vocals, bass, synthes; *Malcolm Holmes*, drums; *Martin Cooper*, keyboards.

Origin:	British
Labels:	*Factory **Dindisc †Telegraph
Top L.P.'s:	**Orchestral Manoeuvres In The Dark (1980), **Organisation (1980), **Architecture & Morality (1981), †Dazzle Ships (1983).
Pick Singles:	*Electricity / Almost (1980), **Red Frame-White Light / I Betray My Friends (1980), **Enola Gay / Annex (1980), **Souvenir / Motion & Heart / Sacred Heart (1981), **Joan Of Arc / Romance Of The Telescope (1981), †Genetic Engineering / 4 Neu (1983), †Telegraph / 66 And Fading (1983).

The Passage   p. 24

North American audiences first met the Passage during 1982 when they supported Richard Strange's Cabaret Futura tour. Pick up a copy of their third and fourth albums, *Degenerates* and *Enflame*, and listen closely to their imaginative blend of drums, oriental chimes, percussion, organ, piano, guitar and voice.

Paul Mahoney, drums; *Andrew Wilson*, guitar, vocals; *Dick Witts*, lead vocals, bass, keyboards.

Origin:	British
Labels:	*Object Music **Night & Day †Cherry Red
Top L.P.'s:	*Pindrop (1980), **For All And None (1981), †Degenerates (1982), †Enflame (1983).
Pick Singles:	*Love Song / Slit Machine (1979), *Time Delay / Sixteen Hours (1979), **Devils & Angels / Watching You Dance (1981), **Troops Out / Hip Rebels (1981), †Taboos / Taboo 'Dub' 12" (1981), †Xoyo / Animal In Me (1982), †Wave / Drugface / Angleland, 12" (1982).

Iggy Pop   p. 119

Born Jim Osterberg, he's better known as Iggy Pop. In 1967 Iggy formed a group called the Stooges, and also moved to Chicago to play drums for several blues groups. The original Stooges split up in 1970, and Iggy reformed the group in 1973 with a new guitarist, James Williamson, to record his third L.P., *Raw Power*, with Mick Ronson and Bowie at the production controls. In 1976 he met David Bowie in California and started recording again. He spent the next few years travelling with Bowie and living in Berlin where he wrote two of his most powerful albums, *The Idiot* and *Lust For Life*. Nowadays Iggy's moved to Brooklyn, New York and is currently signed to Chris (Blondie) Stein's Animal Records. Last year he published his autobiography *I Need More*, a fascinating collection of vignettes and short stories about his childhood and experiences with the Stooges.

Origin:	American
Labels:	*Elektra **Columbia †RCA ††Arista ‡Animal
Top L.P.'s:	*The Stooges (1969), *Funhouse (1970), **Raw Power (1973), †The Idiot (1977), †Lust For Life (1977), ††New Values (1979), ††Soldier (1980), ††Party (1981), ‡Zombie Birdhouse (1982).
Recent Singles:	††I'm Bored / African Man (1979), ††Five Foot One (1979), ††Loco Mosquito / Take Care Of Me (1980), ‡Run Like A Villain / Platonic (1982).

Psychedelic Furs p. 55

Vocalist Richard Butler and his fellow Furs' debut album virtually "ached" with brutal elegance, soul, passion, and despair when it was originally released in 1980. During the summer of '82 the Furs recorded their third L.P., *Forever Now*, at Todd Rundgren's studio in Woodstock, New York. This particular album marked a drastic change from the Furs' previous aggressive, metallic fervor. The single *Love My Way* proved to be a very stunning, atmospheric torch song for the '80s. Original members — saxophonist Duncan Kilburn, guitarist Roger Morris and eventually drummer Vince Ely — left the band to pursue solo careers. Phil Calvert, former drummer for the Birthday Party, replaced Ely.

Richard Butler, vocals; *Phil Calvert*, drums; *John Ashton*, guitar; *Tim Butler*, bass.

Origin:	*British*
Label:	*Epic*
Top L.P.'s:	*Psychedelic Furs* (1980), *Talk Talk Talk* (1981), *Forever Now* (1982).
Pick Singles:	*We Love You / Pulse* (1979), *Sister Europe / Untitled* (1980), *Mr. Jones / Susan's Strange* (1980), *Dumb Waiters / Dash* (1981), *Pretty In Pink / Mack The Knife* (1981), *Love My Way / Aeroplane* (1982), *Danger / Don't Want To Be Your Shadow* (1982).

Public Image Limited p. 108

Since their inception in 1978, after the demise of the Sex Pistols, Public Image Ltd. has pushed the responsibilities of the so-called pop group to new heights. At this point in time PiL are a three-piece consisting of John Lydon, Keith Levene, and drummer Martin Atkins. Former bassist Pete Jones recently left the organization. Their forthcoming album *(You Are Now Entering A) Commercial Zone* should be released in August or September of 1983. Meanwhile, Japanese audiences will get their first taste of PiL when they tour the Orient in June of 1983.

Martin Atkins, drums; *John Lydon*, vocals; *Keith Levene*, guitar, synthes.

Origin:	*British*
Labels:	**Virgin **Virgin / Warner Brothers*
Top L.P.'s:	**First Edition* (1978), **Metal Box (U.S. release titled **Second Edition)* (1979), **Paris au Printemps* (1980), ***Flowers Of Romance* (1981).
Pick Singles:	**Public Image / The Cowboy Song* (1978), **Death Disco / No Birds Do Sing* (1979), **Memories / Another* (1979), **Flowers Of Romance / Home Is Where The Heart Is* (1981).

Pulsallama p. 94

The intriguing aspect of this all-girl group from New York City is that they don't know how to play their instruments that well. The point is they don't have to — they're a parody of the pop female performer spiced by a wacky sense of humor — *Zula rampage in the heart of the concrete jungle.*

Miss April Palmieri, vocals, percussion; *Princess Davis*, vocals, percussion; *Judy Streng*, bass; *Wendy Wild*, glockenspiel, vocals, percussion; *Jean Caffeine*, drums; *Stace "Timbalina" Elkin*, timbalis, cowbells, bass; *Min "Bonefinder" Thometz*, bongos, bass, vocals.

Origin:	*American*
Label:	*Y*
Top L.P.'s:	*The Birth of Y*, a compilation featuring Pulsallama's *Ungawa Part Two* (1982).
Pick Singles:	*Ungawa Pt. 2 (Way Out Guiana) / The Devil Lives In My Husband's Body* (1982), *Qui Qui (A Canadian In Paris) / Pulsallama On The Rag* (1983).

Pylon p. 91

Have you ever seen Pylon perform in concert? If you haven't, then you're missing out on one of life's better offerings, this four-piece pop group from Athens, Georgia. Pylon admit they play "Temporary Rock" as opposed to contemporary. In other words they're playing music for NOW, not for before or after. Like Mike Lachowski says, "We're serious about our music, we just don't take it that seriously." The group recently finished recording the long-overdue second album, *Chomp*, produced by former members of the American pop group, the DB's.

Curtis Crowe, drums; *Randy Bewley*, guitar; *Vanessa Briscoe*, vocals; *Michael Lachowski*, bass.

Origin:	*American*
Labels:	**Caution **Armageddon †DB*
Top L.P.'s:	***Gyrate* (1980), *†Chomp* (1983).
Pick Singles:	**Cool / Dub* (1979), ***Pylon 10" E.P. featuring Cool / Dub / Driving School / Danger* (1980), *†Crazy / M-Train* (1981), *†Beep / Altitude* (1982).

Joey Ramone p. 80

Though the Ramones are probably best-known for the high-intensity garage rock that made them popular in '77, they've gone through transitional stages including the movie *Rock'n'Roll High School* and an album produced by the legendary Phil Spector. Now they're back with their eighth album, *Subterranean Jungle*, featuring renditions of two '60s hits — The Music Explosion's *Little Bit O'Soul* and The Chambers Brothers' *Time Has Come Today.*

Dee Dee Ramone, bass, vocals; *Marky Ramone*, drums; *Johnny Ramone*, guitar; *Joey Ramone*, lead vocals.

Origin:	*American*
Label:	*Sire*
Top L.P.'s:	*The Ramones* (1976), *Leave Home* (1976), *Rocket To Russia* (1977), *Road To Ruin* (1978), *It's Alive* (1979), *End of The Century* (1980), *Pleasant Dreams* (1981), *Subterranean Jungle* (1983).
Pick Singles:	*Blitzkrieg Bop / Havana Affair* (1976), *I Wanna Be Your Boyfriend / California Sun* (1976), *Rockaway Beach / Locket Love* (1977),

Sheena Is A Punk Rocker / I Don't Care (1977), *Do You Wanna Dance? / Long Way Back To Germany* (1978), *Rock'n'Roll High School / Do You Wanna Dance?* "live" (1979), *Do You Remember Rock'n'Roll Radio? / Let's Go* (1980), *We Want The Airwaves / All's Quiet On The Eastern Front* (1981).

Red Decade   p. 134

What would happen if you were to combine jazz phrasing in rhythm, a minimalist technique of composition with a rock'n'roll vocabulary? The answer: *Red Decade*. Decade composer/guitarist Jules Baptiste has played with some of the best avant-garde sound artists in New York — Glenn Branca, Rhys Chatham and Laurie Anderson. Interestingly enough, he contributed all the guitar arrangements on Anderson's original recording of *O' Superman*.

Jules Baptiste, lead guitar; *Fritz Van Orden*, alto sax; *Brian Hudson*, drums; *Jeffery Glenn*, bass.

Origin:	American
Labels:	*Neutral **Noise Fest
Recordings:	*Native Dance / Red Decade, 12" E.P. (1982). **Cleveland Confidential. Compilation L.P. featuring Scars Of Lust "Live" (1982).

The Revillos   p. 33

This zany pop group first assaulted innocent teens with their debut single *Can't Stand My Baby* (1977). Back then they were called the Rezillos. In 1979 the group severed ties with Sire Records, changed the "Z" to "V", and signed a deal with Dindisc. Now they've formed their own record company, *Superville*.

Fay Fife, vocals; *Eugene Reynolds*, vocals; *Kid Krupa*, guitar; *Vince Spik*, bass; *Rocky Rhythm*, drums; and the *Revettes*, backing vocals.

Origin:	Scottish
Labels:	*Sensible **Sire †Dindisc ††Psycho ‡Superville ‡‡Aura
Top L.P.'s:	**Can't Stand The Rezillos (1978), **Mission Accomplished (1979), †Rev Up (1980), ††Teen Beat, 12" E.P. featuring Hip City / Santa Claus Is Coming To Town / 1982 Make A Wish and more (1981), ‡Attack! (1982).
Pick Singles:	*I Can't Stand My Baby / I Wanna Be Your Man (1977), **Destination Venus / Mystery Action (1978), †Motor Bike Beat / No Such Luck (1980), †Scuba Scuba / Scuba Boy Bop (1980), ‡She's Fallen In Love With A Monster Man / Mind Bending Cutie Doll (1981), ‡Bongo Brain / Hip City / You Were Meant For Me (1981), ‡‡Tell Him / Graveyard Groove (1982).

Romeo Void   p. 132

San Francisco never sounded so good. This remarkable five-piece group first came to recognition when Cars' mainman Ric Ocasek produced their controversial dance-floor single *Never Say Never*. Vocalist Debora Iyall has a dynamic, seductive stage presence and is one of America's more sensitive lyricists.

Debora Iyall, vocals; *Peter Woods*, guitar; *Benjamin Bossi*, saxophones; *Frank Zincavage*, bass; *Larry Carter*, drums/percussion.

Origin	American
Labels:	*415 **415/CBS
Top L.P.'s:	*It's A Condition (1981), **Benefactor (1982).
Pick Singles:	*White Sweater / Apache (1981), *Not Safe / Success Story (1981), *Never Say Never, 12" E.P. featuring In The Dark, Present Tense, Not Safe (1981), **Never Say Never / Guards, 7" (1982).

Rough Trade   p. 48

Formed in 1974, Rough Trade has attracted considerable attention in Canada, Australia, Denmark and Holland. Kevan Staples and Carole Pope have four albums to their credit. They've written soundtrack music for *Cruising*, William Friedkin's controversial murder/mystery movie set in the gay leather bars of New York. Several of their songs have also been recorded by Rocky Horror's *Tim Curry*, Germany's *Inga Rumpf*, ex-Labelle vocalist *Nona Hendryx*, and most recently *Dusty Springfield*.

Carole Pope, vocals; *Kevan Staples*, guitar, piano, synthesizer; *Jørn Andersen*, drums; *Howard Ayee*, bass; and *David McMorrow*, keyboards.

Origin:	Canadian
Labels:	*Umbrella **True North
Top L.P.'s:	*Rough Trade "Live" (1976), **Avoid Freud (1980), **For Those Who Think Young (1981), **Shaking The Foundations (1982).
Pick Singles:	**High School Confidential / Grade-B Movie (1981), **It's A Jungle / Lie Back And Let Me Do Everything (1981), **Bodies In Collision / Bloodlust (1982), **All Touch / Baptism Of Fire (1982), **Crimes Of Passion / Endless Night (1983).

Pete Shelley   p. 90

Pete Shelley, best remembered as the singer/songwriter and guitarist for the Manchester-based Buzzcocks, originally formed the group in early '76 with original vocalist Howard Devoto. Eventually, Shelley took over vocals after Devoto went off to form his own group, Magazine. Shelley left the group in '81 to pursue a solo career with England's top electronic record producer, Martin Rushent. Like New Order, Pete Shelley's new-found love for electronics and digital recording may have turned off a lot of his old fans, but he's also won a lot of new ones.

Origin:	British
Labels:	*United Artists **I.R.S. †Genetic

Top L.P.'s:	*Another Music In A Different Kitchen (1978), *Love Bites (1978), **Singles Going Steady (1979), *A Different Kind Of Tension (1979), †Homosapien (1981), †XL.1 (1983).
Solo Singles:	†Homosapien / Keats' Song (1981), †I Don't Know What It Is / Witness The Change (1981), †Telephone Operator / Many A Time (1983), †No One Like You / If You Ask Me (I Won't Say No) (1983).

Shriekback   p. 131

Their sound is loose, instinctual and absorbing. Barry Andrews used to play keyboards for the League of Gentlemen, Iggy Pop, and XTC. Dave Allen gives Shriekback the same thick, seductive bass lines that made the Gang of Four's sound so unique. And Carl Marsh, formerly of Out On Blue Six, now plays guitar for Shriekback and contributes cool, suspenseful vocals. Shriekback are the definitive British groove band of '83.

Carl Marsh, guitar, lead vocals; *Dave Allen,* bass; *Barry Andrews,* keyboards, percussion; *Pedro Ortiz,* percussion; *Martyn Barker,* drums.

Origin:	*British*
Label:	*Y*
Top L.P.'s:	*The Birth Of Y,* a compilation L.P. featuring *Despite Dense Weed* (1982), *Tench,* 12" E.P. (1982), *Care* (1983).
Pick Singles:	*Sexthinkone / Here Comes My Handclap (1982), My Spine Is The Bassline / Tiny Birds (1982), Lined Up / Hapax Legomena (1983), Working On The Ground,* 12" mix (1983).

Simple Minds   p. 8

This Glasgow-based pop group debuted with *Life In A Day* (1979), and their sound was very rock'n'roll oriented. The big change came with their second album, *Real To Real Cacophony,* when they dropped their rock approach in favor of a much more hypnotic electro-dance beat. Their fine fourth album *Sons & Fascination,* scored two impressive dance-floor hits, *The American* and *Love Song.* Their most recent album, *New Gold Dream (81-82-83-84),* has been doing equally as well with the singles *Promised You A Miracle* and *Glittering Prize.*

Charles Burchill, guitar; *Derek Forbes,* bass; *Michael MacNeil,* keyboards; *Jim Kerr,* vocals; *Mel Gaynor,* drums.

Origin:	*Scottish*
Labels:	**Zoom / Arista **Virgin*
Top L.P.'s:	**Life In A Day (1979), *Real To Real Cacophony (1979), *Empires & Dance (1980), **Sons & Fascination / Sister Feelings Call (1981), **New Gold Dream (81-82-83-84) (1982).*
Pick Singles:	**Chelsea Girl / Garden Of Hate (1979), *Changeling / Premonition "live" (1979), *I Travel / New Warm Skin (1980), **The American / League Of Nations (1981), **Love Song / This Earth That You Walk Upon (1981), **Promised You A Miracle / Theme For Great Cities (1982), **Glittering Prize / Glittering Prize "Theme" (1982).*

Siouxsie and the Banshees (The Creatures)   p. 23

The Banshees are one of the only surviving groups, with the exception of the Clash, to come out of the '77 British punk explosion. Siouxsie Sioux has been voted top female vocalist for the third consecutive year by the *New Musical Express* Reader's Poll. The two founding members, bassist Steve Severin and Sioux, are the main songwriting force. Robert Smith of the Cure recently joined the Banshees as their permanent guitarist, replacing John McGeoch. A variety of solo projects are likely to appear on their new Wonderland label in the near future, and among them is a new debut album by the Creatures, a two-piece group formed by Sioux and drummer Budgie. In 1981 the Creatures released the controversial *Wild Things E.P.,* and their debut album, recorded in Hawaii, is called *Feast.*

Steve Severin, bass; *Siouxsie Sioux,* vocals; *Budgie,* drums; *Robert Smith,* guitar.

Origin:	*British*
Labels:	**Polydor **Wonderland / Polydor*
Top L.P.'s:	**The Scream (1978), *Join Hands (1979), *Kaleidoscope (1980), *Ju Ju (1981), *A Kiss In The Dreamhouse (1982), **Feast (a solo project by the Creatures) (1983).*
Pick Singles:	**Hong Kong Garden / Voices (1978), *The Staircase (Mystery) / 20th Century Boy (1979), *Happy House / Drop Dead — Celebration (1980), *Christine / Eve White / Eve Black (1980), *Israel / Red Over White (1980), *Spellbound / Follow The Sun (1981), *Slowdrive / Cannibal Roses (1982), *Melt! / Il Est Ne Le Devin Enfant (1982), **Miss The Girl / Hot Springs In The Snow (the Creatures 1983).*

Sparks   p. 62

The nucleus of Sparks, brothers Ron and Russell Mael, are probably best known for their 1974 hit album *Kimono My House.* They've recorded over twelve albums and have been signed to seven different major labels. They shocked fans in '79 when they recorded an all-electronic dance album, *No 1 In Heaven,* with Giorgio Moroder, the producer who made Donna Summer a disco sensation. Sparks were several years ahead of their time, and recently the Human League and similar bands have acknowledged Sparks as a major influence.

Russell Mael, vocals; *Ron Mael,* synthesizers, keyboards.

Origin:	*American*
Labels:	**Island **CBS †Elektra ††Why-Fi ‡Atlantic ‡‡Virgin*
Top L.P.'s:	**Kimono My House (1974), *Propaganda (1974), *Indiscreet (1975), **Big Beat (1976),*

***Introducing Sparks* (1977), †‡‡*No 1 In Heaven* (1979), ††*Whomp That Sucker* (1981), ‡*Angst In My Pants* (1982), ‡*Sparks In Outer Space* (1983).

Recent Singles: †*Tips For Teens / Don't Shoot Me* (1981), ‡‡*Young Girls / Just Because You Love Me* (1980), ‡*I Predict / Moustache* (1982), ‡*Cool Places / Sports* (1983).

Chris Spedding — p. 100

Chris Spedding is the supreme guitar virtuoso; he has played with some of the best artists of our time, including John Cale and Roxy Music, and produced everybody from the Sex Pistols to Snips. Originally guitarist for The Sharks in the early '70's, Spedding eventually went solo, landed a recording contract with RAK Records with the legendary Mickie Most at the production controls. He's currently in New York City.

Origin: British
Labels: *RAK **Passport
Top L.P.'s: *Chris Spedding (1976), *Hurt (1977), *Guitar Graffiti (1978), **I'm Not Like Everybody Else* (1980), **Friday The 13th (1981).
Pick Singles: **Pogo Dancing / The Pose* (1976), **Get Outa My Pagoda / Hey Miss Betty* (1977), **Bored Bored / Time Warp* (1978), **Gunfight / Evil* (1978), **The Crying Game / Counterfeit* (1980).

Spoons — p. 68

They come from a small commuter town called Burlington, west of Toronto, and in 1982 their phenomenal second album, *Arias & Symphonies*, touched the hearts of thousands of teenagers across Canada. Groups of the Spoons' calibre are certainly providing new alternatives to the predominantly Canadian heavy metal scene when it comes to originality, self-expression and style.

Derrick Ross, drums, percussion; *Sandy Horne*, bass, vocals; *Rob Preuss*, keyboards, synthes; *Gordon Deppe*, lead vocals, guitar.

Origin: Canadian
Labels: *Mannequin **Ready †*Ready / A&M*
Top L.P.'s: ***Stick Figure Neighbourhood* (1981), †*Arias & Symphonies* (1982).
Pick Singles: **After The Institution / My Job* (1980), †*Nova Heart / Symmetry* (1982), ***Arias & Symphonies / Trade Winds* (1982), ***Smiling In Winter / South American Vacation* (1983).

Steel Pulse — p. 122

The majority of Pulse originated from Handsworth, a small borough of Birmingham, England. They recorded their first single *Kibudu, Mansetta And Abuku* during late '76 on their first independent label *Dip*. The group's popularity grew rapidly when they released their second single, *Nyah Love*. Probably the group's biggest single to date is the controversial *Ku Klux Klan* anthem, their first for Island Records. Now, after four albums, and several memorable appearances at Reggae Sunsplash '81, Steel Pulse are busy recording their follow-up L.P. to *True Democracy*.

Victor Yesufu, lead guitar; *Steve "Grizzly" Nesbitt*, drums; *Phonso Martin*, percussion, vocals; *Selwyn "Bumbo" Brown*, keyboards, vocals; *Ronald "Stepper" McQueen*, bass; *David Hinds*, lead vocals, rhythm guitar.

Origin: British
Labels: *Anchor ***Island / Mango* †*Elektra / WEA*
Top L.P.'s: ***Handsworth Revolution* (1978), ***Tribute To The Martyrs* (1979), **Reggae Fever (1980), ***Reggae Sunsplash '81* (1982), †*True Democracy* (1982).
Pick Singles: *Nyah Love (1977), **Ku Klux Klan (1978), ***Prediction / Revolution Dub "Take Two" / Maka*, 12" (1978), ***Sound System / Babylon Makes The Rules / Devil's Disciples*, 12" (1979).

Sting — p. 93

Six years ago Gordon Sumner (aka Sting) was the bassist/vocalist for the Police, an obscure reggae/punk trio that didn't fare too well with the British music scene. Now, six years later, he's become a pop idol and actor (*Quadrophenia, Brimstone and Treacle*). Looking back, it's interesting to see what an impact the Police's music (their unique blend of white roots reggae and pop) has had on the current state of commercial pop, i.e., Men At Work.

Origin: British
Labels: *Illegal ***A&M* †*Island*
Top L.P.'s: ***Outlandos D'Amour* (1978), **Regatta De Blanc (1979), ***Zenyatta Mondatta* (1980), ***Ghost In The Machine* (1981), †*The Secret Policeman's Other Ball* (includes acoustic versions of *Roxanne* and *Message In A Bottle*) (1982), ***Brimstone & Treacle Music From The Original Soundtrack* (1982), **Synchronicity (1983).
Pick Singles: **Fall Out / Nothing Achieving* (1977), ***Roxanne / Peanuts* (1978), ***Message In A Bottle / Landlord* (1979), ***Don't Stand So Close To Me / Friends* (1980), ***Every Little Thing She Does Is Magic / Flexible Strategies* (1981), ***Spread A Little Happiness / Only You* (1982), ***Every Breath You Take / Murder By Numbers* (1983).

Richard Strange — p. 117

Performance art, mime, dance, comedy, poetry and video installations — these are just a few of the things former Doctors of Madness vocalist, Richard Strange (aka Kid Strange), has been promoting. You may remember him from the London-based *Cabaret Futura*, a mixed media nightclub that steered away from the traditional rock format. Unlike most groups who use pre-recorded tapes in their live shows, Strange doesn't use a backing band when he's performing. A reel-to-reel tape recorder is placed in clear view, and Richard sings from the heart, with such conviction, that you don't even care if the music isn't being played live. He recently made his acting debut in the British animated film *Duet*, with sound track by Neil Arthur of Blancmange.

Origin: British
Labels: *Polydor **Cherry Red †ZE ††Virgin ‡Interslam
Top L.P.'s: *Figments of Emancipation (1976), *Late Night Movies, All Night Brainstorms (1976), *Sons of Survival (1978), †The Live Rise of Richard Strange (1980), ††The Phenomenal Rise of Richard Strange (1981), ††Cabaret Futura featuring Fools Rush In Where Angels Dare to Tread (1981).
Pick Singles: **International Language / Kiss Tomorrow Goodbye (1980), ††International Language / God Is Science (1981), ††The Phenomenal Rise of Richard Strange / On Top of the World (1981), ‡Next, 12" E.P. (1983).

The Stranglers p. 133

Since they first introduced themselves to British audiences in 1976 with *Down In The Sewer* and *Get A Grip On Yourself*, the Stranglers have never ceased exploring new territory. Their most recent studio effort, *Feline*, was written, rehearsed and recorded in Brussels. Recently, the Stranglers experienced considerable success in Europe with their ballad-oriented singles — *Golden Brown*, *Strange Little Girl* and *European Female*. Now they're prophesizing *Aural Sculpture*, a "maninblackfesto" that conveys a new breed of musical appreciation and interpretation.

J.J. Burnel, bass, vocals; *Dave Greenfield*, keyboards, synthes; *Jet Black*, drums, percussion; *Hugh Cornwell*, vocals, electric and acoustic guitars.

Origin: British / Swedish / French
Labels: *United Artists **Liberty †Epic
Top L.P.'s: *Rattus Norvegicus (1977), *No More Heroes (1977), *Black & White (1978), *The Raven (1979), **The Meninblack (1980), **La Folie (1981, †Feline (1983).
Pick Singles: *(Get A) Grip (On Yourself) / Hanging Around (1977), *Nice'n'Sleazy / Shut Up (1978), *Nuclear Device / Yellowcake UF 6 (1979), *Bear Cage / Shah Shah A Go Go (1980), **Golden Brown / Love 30 (1982), **Strange Little Girl / Cruel Garden (1982), †European Female / Savage Breast (1982), †Midnight Summer Dream / Vladimir & Olga (1983).

Stray Cats p. 32

When the Stray Cats first started gigging in their native New York, nobody wanted to have anything to do with them, let alone their rockabilly rhythms. In 1979 the trio moved to London and eventually recorded two albums and several singles for Arista Records. Two years after *Rock This Town* and *Stray Cat Strut* were released in Europe (circa 1981), the very same songs became smash hits in North America in 1983.

Slim Jim Phantom, snare drum; *Lee Rocker*, slap bass; *Brian Setzer*, guitar, vocals.

Origin: American
Labels: *Arista (U.K.) **EMI America
Top L.P.'s: *Stray Cats (1981), *Gonna Ball (1981), **Built For Speed (U.S. compilation) (1982).
Pick Singles: *Runaway Boys / My One Desire (1980), *Rock This Town / Can't Hurry Love (1981), *Stray Cat Strut / Drink That Bottle Down (1981), *You Don't Believe Me / Cross That Bridge (1981), *Little Miss Prissy / Sweet Love On My Mind / Something Else "live" (1981).

The Style Council p. 89

Fellow Councillor vocalist/guitarist Paul Weller is probably best remembered as the mastermind behind Britain's most cherished pop group, the political voice for English youth — the Jam. Now Weller fronts the Style Council, a two-piece that also features the talented Mick Talbot on keyboards. Weller's new sound is extremely r&b oriented, highly reminiscent of the '60s Stax and Motown sound. In March of '83 the Style Council's debut single, *Speak Like A Child*, skyrocketed straight into the British Top Ten and stayed there for several weeks. When asked about the possibility of an album, Weller announced that he had no immediate plans for a Style Council album, and that he'd much prefer to concentrate on producing good quality singles.

Mick Talbot, keyboards; *Paul Weller*, vocals, guitar.

Origin: British
Label: Polydor
Top L.P.'s: Debut L.P. not yet released.
Pick Singles: Speak Like A Child / Party Chambers (1983), Money Go Round (Parts 1 and 2) / Head Start To Happiness / Mick's Up, 12" E.P. (1983).

Bernard Szajner p. 98

Szajner, originally of Polish descent, first decided to combine his experience as an audio-visual technician with electronic music. Now, with three experimental electronic albums to his credit, Szajner has just completed his fourth L.P., *Brute Reason*. Howard Devoto, former vocalist for the now defunct British pop group Magazine, flew to Paris to write lyrics and sing lead vocals on three of the tracks. However, it is Szajner's invention of his two laser instruments, *The Laser Harp* and *The Snark*, which will make him a revolutionary force in the future of popular music and its ever-changing technology.

Origin: *French*
Labels: **Initial Recording Company / EMI-Pathe Marconi **Initial Recording Company †Island*
Top L.P.'s: **Visions Of Dune (1978), *Some Deaths Take Forever (1981), **Superficial Music (1982), †Brute Reason (1983).*

Taxi Girl p. 103

Suicide Romeo, Taxi Girl and Marquis de Sade were a few of the more popular punk groups to emerge from the French underground, about 1977-78. Now, five years later, the only group still recording are Taxi Girl. After recording two E.P.'s for Pathé Marconi, the band finally recorded their 1981 debut L.P., Seppuku, for Virgin Records. Stranglers' bassist J.J. Burnel produced it and Jet Black played drums. Seppuku proved to be an enormous breakthrough for French pop, both musically and stylistically. Since the departure of original keyboardist Laurent Sinclair, Taxi Girl are currently a two-piece and they've just finished recording their most recent 12" E.P., Cette Fille Est Une Erreur.

Daniel (Darc) Rozoum, lead vocals; *Mir Wais*, guitar; *Jean-Marc*, keyboards; *Philippe*, bass; *Fabrice*, drums.

Origin: *French*
Labels: **EMI / Pathé Marconi **Mankin / Virgin*
Top L.P.'s: ***Seppuku (1981), **Cette Fille Est Une Erreur, 12" six-track E.P. (1983).*
Pick Singles: **Manequin / Triste Cocktail / Les Yeux Des Amants (1979), *Cherchez Le Garcon / Jardin Chinois / V2 Sur Mes Souvenirs (1980), **La Femme Escarlate / Musée Tong (1981), **Les Armées De La Nuit / Elégie (1981).*

Telephone p. 30

"Before 1976 there was no rock'n'roll in France," explains Telephone's chief songwriter/vocalist Jean-Louis Aubert. "The paradox was that a whole generation in America and Britain grew up listening to rock. That's why I decided to do something about it with my friends. The logical thing to do was to form a group." In 1977 Telephone were the very first rock band to come out of France. Their success was significant because it was the first time the French language merged with the rock vocabulary. Telephone are a straightforward, energetic, no-frills rock band. Their most recent album, Dure Limite, sold over 500,000 copies in France within the first six months of release.

Jean-Louis Aubert, vocals, guitar; *Corinne Marienneau*, bass; *Louis Bertignac*, guitar, vocals; *Richard Kolinka*, drums.

Origin: *French*
Labels: **EMI / Pathé Marconi **Virgin*
Top L.P.'s: **Telephone (1977), *Crache Ton Venin (1979), *Au Coeur De La Nuit (1980), **Dure Limite (1982).*
Pick Singles: **La Bombe Humaine / J'suis Parti De Chez Mes Parents (1979), *J'sais Tasp Quoi Faire / La Bombe Humaine (1980), *Argent Trop Cher / Au Coeur De La Nuite (1981), *Le Silence / Un Peu De Ton Amour / Fleur De Ma Ville / Prends Ce Que Tu Veux (1981), **Ca (C'est Vraiment Toi) / Serrez (1982), **Cendrillon / Ex Robin Des Bois (1982).*

David Thomas p. 115

Initially called Foggy & the Shrimps, Cleveland, Ohio's avant-garde/experimental band Pere Ubu first recorded music on their own independent Hearthan label in 1975. David Thomas, sometimes referred to as Crocus Behemoth, was the main guiding light, vocalist and singer/songwriter behind Ubu, and even though they no longer exist as a legitimate working band, Thomas is still recording albums as a solo artist under the unusual name of David Thomas and his Legs.

Origin: *American*
Labels: **Hearthan **Blank †Chrysalis ††Rough Trade ‡Recommended*
Top L.P's.: ***The Modern Dance (1978), †Dub Housing (1978), †New Picnic Time (1979), ††Art Of Walking (1980), ††390 Degrees Of Simulated Stereo (1981), ††Song Of The Bailing Man (1982), ††The Sound Of Sand (by D. Thomas and the Pedestrians 1982), ‡Winter Comes Home (1983).*
Pick Singles: **30 Seconds Over Toyko / Heart Of Darkness (1975), *Final Solution / Cloud 149 (1976), *Modern Dance / Heaven (1977), †The Fabulous Sequel (Have Shoes, Will Walk) / Humor Me "live" / The Book Is On The Table (1979), ††Not Happy / Lonesome Dave (1981), ††D. Thomas — Vocal Performances, 12" E.P. featuring Petrified and Sloop John B. (1982).*

Thompson Twins p. 10

When the Thompson Twins were first introduced to the pop scene in their native England in 1977, they were, as vocalist Tom Bailey professes, "An experimental cult group." These days the Twins have trimmed down their original line-up of seven to three. Now the sound places emphasis on keyboards, bass, and percussion, deliberately avoiding their traditional guitar format. Their initial success came from the single In The Name Of Love, which shot up to the number one position in the Rockpool charts (America's official club chart) during the summer of 1982. Since then the revamped, new and improved Twins are riding the crest of the wave with their latest singles Lies, Love On Your Side, and We Are Detective.

Joe Leeway, congas, synthes, vocals; *Alannah Currie*, xylophone, percussion, vocals; *Tom Bailey*, vocals, synthes, drum programmes.

Origin: *British (Currie's from New Zealand)*
Labels: **Latent **T / Arista †Arista*

Top L.P.'s:	**A Product of...(1981), **Set (1982), †Quick Step and Side Kick (Side Kicks) (1983).
Pick Singles:	*She's In Love With Mystery / Fast Food — Food Style (1980), **Perfect Game / Politics (1980), **Make Believe (Let's Pretend) / Lama Sabach Tani (1981), **Animal Laugh / Anything Is Good Enough (1981), **In The Name Of Love / In The Beginning (1982), **Runaway / Bouncing (1982), †Lies / Beach Culture (1982), †Love On Your Side / Instrumental (1983), †We Are Detective / Lucky Day (1983).

U2   p. 135

This Irish group's third and most recent album, *War*, is a major achievement. Although their previous album, *October*, didn't fare too well with the critics, *War* inherits the same kind of freshness and vitality that their debut *Boy* did. On *War* U2 showcase a variety of styles and they even go as far as to use female backing vocals on a few tracks. U2 have proved they can write consistently moving music with a feel and understanding for today's youth.

Bono, vocals; *The Edge*, guitar; *Adam Clayton*, bass; *Larry Mullen*, drums.

Origin:	Irish
Labels:	*CBS **Island
Top L.P.'s:	* **Boy (1980), * **October (1981), * **War (1983).
Pick Singles:	*Another Day / Twilight (1980), * **11 O'Clock Tick Tock / Touch (1980), * **I Will Follow / Boy Girl (1980), * **Fire / J. Swallo (1981), * **Gloria / I Will Follow "live" (1981), * **A Celebration / Trash, Trampoline and the Party Girl (1982), * **New Year's Day / Treasure (Whatever Happened to Pete the Chop) (1983), * **Two Hearts Beat As One / Endless Deep (1983).

James Blood Ulmer   p. 83

Guitarist James Blood Ulmer comes from the Ornette Coleman school of harmolotic music; in fact, he used to play for Ornette. Ulmer is paving the way for jazz-rock fusion by modulating between funk, rock, r&b and jazz simultaneously. Although Blood's band is usually a trio — Grant Calvin Weston on drums and Amin Ali on electric bass — his most recent album, *Black Rock*, features a second guitarist, Ronnie Drayton.

James Blood Ulmer, (alias *Damu Mustafa Abdul Musawwir*), guitar, vocals; *Amin Ali*, electric bass; *Grant Calvin Weston*, drums.

Origin:	American
Labels:	*Artist's House **Rough Trade †CBS
Top L.P.'s:	*Tales Of Captain Black (1979), **Are You Glad To Live In America? (1980), †Freelancing (1981), †Black Rock (1982).

Alan Vega   p. 56

Originally the vocal half of New York's first electronic avant-garde punk group, Suicide (circa '76), Vega, along with keyboard wiz Martin Rev, made the rhythm machine a legitimate instrument. Suicide, along with the New York Dolls and Wayne County, came out of the Mercer Arts Centre/Max's Kansas City club scene in the mid '70s. Current British electronic groups like Soft Cell and Blancmange have even adapted Suicide's original two-man format. Now a solo artist, his current sound is a (per) version of rockabilly. Though he's a native New Yorker, Vega's first two solo albums, *Alan Vega* and *Collision Drive*, virtually made him an overnight sensation in France and Belgium. His latest effort, *Saturn Strip*, was produced by Ric Ocasek of the Cars.

Origin:	American
Labels:	*Max **Red Star †Bronze ††ZE/ Celluloid ‡Elektra
Top L.P.'s:	*Max's Kansas City '76 (1976), **Suicide (1977), ††Alan Vega — Martin Rev (1980), ††Alan Vega (1980), ††A Christmas Album featuring Suicide's Hey Lord (1981), ††Collision Drive (1981), ‡Saturn Strip (1983).
Pick Singles:	†Cheree / I Remember (1978), ††Dream Baby Dream / Radiation (1979), ††Jukebox Babe/ Love Cry (1980), ††Magdalena 82 / Magdalena 83 (1981), ‡Video Babe, 12" E.P. (1983).

Tom Verlaine   p. 26

Verlaine played guitar in the Neon Boys, a group that he formed with Richard Hell in 1973. Come 1974, Hell split and the Neon Boys changed their name to Television. Since the group's demise in 1978, Verlaine decided to pursue a solo career. He's recorded three solo L.P.'s, but none of them have really been big commercial successes. Verlaine's next solo album will feature keyboards as well as guitars. Call him the genius of future pop.

Origin:	American
Labels:	*Elektra **Warner Brothers †Ork ††Virgin
Top L.P.'s:	*Marquee Moon (1977), *Adventure (1978), *Tom Verlaine (1979), **Dreamtime (1981), ** ††Words From The Front (1982).
Pick Singles:	†Little Johnny Jewel (Parts 1 & 2) (1975), *Prove It / Venus (1977), *Foxhole / Careful (1978), *Glory / Ain't That Nothin' (1978), **Always / The Blue Rose (1981), ††Postcard From Waterloo / Clear It Away (1982).
Cassette:	The Blow Up, Television "live" 1978 (Roir Cassettes, 1983).

Holly Beth Vincent p. 81

You may recall Holly and Joey Ramone's classic rendition of Sonny and Cher's *I Got You Babe* in the import bins during 1982. If Joey ever decides to record a solo album, Holly will most likely be playing guitar on it. Recently, during April of 1983, Holly finally disbanded the Italians. She is currently singing lead vocals for the Waitresses *(I Know What Boys Like)*, replacing original singer Patty Donahue.

Origin: American
Labels: *Oval **Virgin
Top L.P.'s: **The Right To Be Italian (1981), **Holly Beth Vincent (1982).
Pick Singles: *Tell That Girl To Shut Up / Chapel Of Love (1980), **Miles Away / It's Only Me (1980), **Youth Coup / Poster Boy (1981), **I Wanna Go Home / Fanzine (1981), **Honalu / Revenge (1982), **For What It's Worth (What's That Sound) / Dangerously (1982).

Wall of Voodoo p. 46

Wall of Voodoo are probably best known for their rendition of the old Johnny Cash hit *Ring Of Fire*, and their most recent self-penned hit *Mexican Radio*, complete with a video which features vocalist Stanard Ridgway popping his head out of a vat of hot, syrupy baked beans. Index Records, the group's original independent label, recently released a 12" E.P. of old live material called *The Morricone Themes* which features renditions of film soundtracks from Clint Eastwood's spaghetti westerns — *Hang Em' High* and *The Good, the Bad and the Ugly*.

Stanard Ridgway, vocals; *Joe Nanini*, drums, percussion; *Chas T. Gray*, synthes; *Bill Noland*, keyboards; *Mark Moreland*, guitar.

Origin: American
Labels: *Index **I.R.S. / Illegal
Top L.P.'s: *12" E.P. Wall Of Voodoo featuring Longarm, The Passenger, Can't Make Love, Struggle, Ring Of Fire and Grandma's House (1980), **Dark Continent (1981), **Call Of The West (1982).
Pick Singles: **Mexican Radio / Call Of The West (1982), **Interstate 15 / Nothing On This Side (1982), *The Morricone Themes featuring Hang 'Em High and The Good, the Bad and the Ugly (both "live") — also includes Ring Of Fire (remix) (1982).

James White and the Blacks alias James Chance and the Contortions p. 47

James White has been a veteran of the New York new music scene dating back to the mid '70s when he first started playing with his first group, *Teenage Jesus and the Jerks*. From there he went on to form the now-legendary *Contortions*, probably New York's most adventurous of rhythmic funk groups. He was playing dance music long before it became popular in the new wave dance clubs of today.

James White, lead vocals, alto sax, electric & acoustic piano, farfisa organ; *Chris Cunningham*, guitar; *Colin Wade*, bass; *Ralph Rolle*, drums, percussion; *Jerry Antonius*, guitar; the *Discolitas*, backing vocals.

Origin: American
Labels: *Ze **Invisible †Animal
Top L.P.'s: *12" E.P. Contort Yourself (Tropical) Heatwave (1978), *Buy Contortions (1979), *Off White (1979), **Live Aux Bains Douches (1980), *12" E.P. Theme From Grutzi Elvis Schleyer's Tires / McGraw Army Base / Munchen / That's When Your Heartache Begins (1979), †Sax Maniac (1982).
Cassette: Live In New York — James Chance And The Contortions (1981, available on ROIR cassettes).

X p. 72

If you lived in L.A. during the late '70s you were probably one of the many punk rockers who frequented Chinatown, the only available outlet for new music. Rockers stormed Madame Wong's, a popular Chinatown punk emporium, to see their favorite groups perform — including the late Darby Crash of the Germs, Black Flag, Alley Cats, and X. Six years later, only X have managed to land a major recording contract. Their sound is intense, threatening, and dramatic. Their records are produced by Ray Manzarek, former keyboard player for the Doors.

Billy Zoom, guitar; *Exene Cervenka*, vocals; *John Doe*, vocals, bass; *D.J. Bonebrake*, drums, marimba.

Origin: American
Labels: *Dangerhouse **Slash †Elektra
Top L.P.'s: *Yes L.A. (1979), **The Decline Of Western Civilization (1980), **Los Angeles (1980), **Wild Gift (1981), †Under The Big Black Sun (1982).
Pick Singles: *Adult Books / We're Desperate (1978), **White Girl / Your Phone's Off The Hook (But You're Not) (1980), †Blue Spark / Dancing With Tears In My Eyes (1982), †The Hungry Wolf.

Yellowman p. 22

During the summer of 1982, Jamaica's premier toaster/rap artist, Yellowman, performed at the fifth annual Reggae Sunsplash as well as the first Jamaican World Music Festival, and stole both shows in the process. Yellowman is probably best known for his "slack" style of rapping. At the moment Yellowman is the toast of Jamaica — funky, humorous and cheeky. He's the undisputed clownprince of reggae rap fever!

Origin: Jamaican
Labels: *Greensleeves **V.P.
Recent Recordings: *Yellowman & Fathead's Bad Boy Skanking (1982), **Duppy or Gunman (1981), *Mister Yellowman (1982), **Live at Aces, Yellowman & Fathead (1981), *The Yellow, the Purple and the Nancy (1982).

Discography complete to May, 1983.